Royal London

THE OFFICIAL LONDON TRANSPORT GUIDE TO EXPLORING LONDON'S HERITAGE

LONDON TRANSPORT

Published jointly by **London Transport, 55 Broadway, Westminster, London SW1** and **Book Production Consultants, 47 Norfolk Street, Cambridge CB1 2LE**

Published 1991.
© London Transport Museum and Book Production Consultants 1991.
ISBN 1 871829 05 4

A CIP catalogue record for this book is available from the British Library.

Whilst every effort has been made to ensure the accuracy of the information contained in this book, the publishers can take no responsibility for possible errors or omissions, and readers should note that changes in admission and travel details occur from time to time. The inclusion of a building or open space in this publication does not necessarily imply the right of entry. The opinions expressed are those of the compiler and are not necessarily those of the publishers.

Enquiries regarding advertising in future editions of this and other guides in the series should be addressed to **Book Production Consultants, 47 Norfolk Street, Cambridge CB1 2LE.**

Other Guides in the series:
Budget London
Family London
London Breaks

The publishers would like to thank the following for their permission to reproduce photographs: pp. 5, 12, 16, 41, 62 (bottom), 83, 104, David Phillips; pp.13, 14 (right), 15, 34 (both), 35, 36, 37, 42, 54, 55 (bottom), 58-9, 80, 82, 95 (top), J C Mervyn Blatch; p.14 (left), National Portrait Gallery; pp.17, 20, By courtesy of the Board of Trustees of the Victoria & Albert Museum; p.19, Harrods Limited; pp.22, 23, Royal Albert Hall; pp.24, 60, 81, 95 (bottom), 96, Crown copyright and reproduced with the permission of the controller of HMSO; p.52, Metropolitan Police; p.55 (top), House of Commons Public Information Office; pp.57,85, Imperial War Museum; p.62 (left and right), The Savoy Group; p.64, London Transport Museum; p.65, Woodmansterne Picture Library; pp.77, 97, The London Tourist Board; p.84 (top and bottom), The Museum of the Moving Image; p.98 (top and bottom), The National Maritime Museum; p.100, The Docklands Development Corporation.

Design and production by **Book Production Consultants**

Based on a previous edition of *Royal & Historic London*, originally published by London Transport. Text completely revised and updated by **Jenny Ward**.

Cover design by **Peter Dolton**
Book design by **Peter Dolton**
Illustrations by **John York**
Maps by **FWT, London N19**
Film origination by **Anglia Graphics, Bedford**
Printed and bound in the United Kingdom by **Staples Printers (Kettering) Ltd.**

CONTENTS

INTRODUCTION

Ships, towers, domes, theatres, and temples lie
Open unto the fields, and to the sky;

wrote Wordsworth on a visit to London
one day in September 1802. Nearly two hundred
years later the skyline displays shapes he would not be
able to identify, but many of the things he did see remain.
There are even traces of the fields he glimpsed from
Westminster Bridge in place-names such as Lincoln's Inn
Fields. London is ever changing, but one thing that does
not change is the abundance of things to see
and enjoy that it offers to visitors.

The four official London Transport guides – *Royal &
Historic London, Budget London, Family London* and
London Breaks – are designed for the visitor to London
who has little time to spare. To get the most out of a short
stay or day trip, choose the book that best suits your
pocket and your needs. *Royal & Historic London* is the
one for those who particularly want to see the traditional
places and events. *Budget London* has lots of suggestions
for enjoying yourself with the minimum outlay; it takes in
all the major tourist attractions in doing that. *Family
London* offers ideas for all ages – and if your group includes someone who is disabled, note that the walks in it
contain specific information for wheelchair users. All the
guides include a Disabled in London section with transport advice.

These tours were originally devised by London jour-
nalist Keith Blogg in the early 1980s and since then they
have been tried and tested by eight million visitors. They
have been completely checked and re-written to bring
them up to date for the 1990s. Each walk can be completed in a day, with some help here and there from buses
and tubes. Follow all four walks in the guide and you will
be sure of seeing all the main features that central London
has to offer. If you prefer to plan your own route, you will
find that the walks are interconnected and that it is easy
for you to switch back and forth between them as you
wish.

What made London great, from Roman times onwards, was its main highway, the Thames. It's no coincidence that most of the sights of London are close to it. The Thames has been coming into its own again in recent years with the development of Docklands. You may like to use the river as a highway in your explorations in the city, or you can mix a river and coach trip to see further afield. Turn to the side trips for ideas.

A brief guide to the ever-changing nightlife of London is included in a separate section. You can experience the atmosphere of London after dark by simply exploring the streets mentioned. If you want to do more than that, you will need up-to-the-minute information to supplement what is given here. Consult the daily papers and specialist weeklies such as *Time Out, City Limits* and *What's On.*

To help you find your way, there is a map for each walk showing the route and the places of interest described. At the end of the guide there is a pull-out map giving you a comprehensive view of the capital city. There are so many things to see in a short distance in central London that sometimes there is too much detail to be shown clearly in the space available on the maps. You will find it useful to have a copy of a detailed plan such as the *London A to Z* to consult alongside the ones supplied here.

Along the top of each of the double-page spreads to the walks, you will find a simplified linear representation of the instructions provided in the text beneath. Be sure to refer to the text and map for directions.

Entrance information is given at the end of each walk, together with phone numbers. It is wise to check a day or so in advance that your main destinations will be open when you plan to visit, especially as sometimes special events can disrupt public access. Opening times and prices are always changing and the details given should be used for general guidance only. For tourist information in office hours the London Tourist Board has a helpline on 071-730 3488.

You may prefer to travel by public transport rather than to walk between the places you visit. If so, make use of the details given about buses and tube stations at the end of each walk. Cafes and toilets are mentioned occasionally where they are thin on the ground, but you will not have any problem in finding these in the centre.

Travel information cannot be guaranteed in advance as London Transport is continually improving routes and services. For travel enquiries dial London Transport on 071-222 1234, or Travelcheck (for recorded, up-to-the-minute information) on 071-222 1200. If you are dialling from a number with the same prefix as the one you need, leave out the prefix. Each of these numbers has a queuing system; if you re-dial you lose your place, so hang on if you don't get a reply at first. There are separate sections towards the end of the guide with more detailed transport and tourist information.

Above all, enjoy your stay, and welcome to London.

KEY

U Nearest Underground station

BR Nearest British Rail station

DLR Nearest Docklands Light Railway station

D Access for the disabled

While you're seeing the sights in Britain don't forget the folks back home. In any language a postcard is the brightest, quickest and simplest way to say Hi!

They take seconds to write and arrive at their destination in no time at all. They are also great value.

Stamps are available in handy books of four which you can carry with you wherever you travel.

Pick up a book from post offices or anywhere you see the Royal Mail Stockist signs.

P.S. *Want to say more? Or say it more personally? Then send a colourful new pictorial aerogramme, available from post offices.*

Royal Mail

International

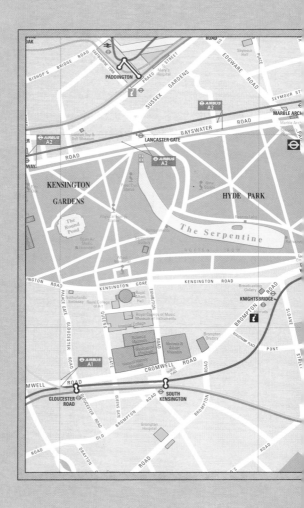

TRAFALGAR SQUARE
NATIONAL GALLERY
BUCKINGHAM PALACE
MUSEUMS
ROYAL ALBERT HALL
KENSINGTON PALACE
MARBLE ARCH

WALK 1

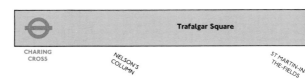

The tube station for Trafalgar Square is Charing Cross, on the Jubilee, Northern and Bakerloo lines. Coming up into the square from the Underground entrance it really does seem that this, if anywhere, is the centre of London. In one sense it is, because near the statue of Charles I on his horse is a bronze plaque marking the spot where distances to London are traditionally measured. This was the original site of Charing Cross, where Eleanor of Castile's funeral procession rested on its way to Westminster Abbey in 1290. She was the *'chère reine'* of Edward I, hence 'Charing'.

Charles I

Trafalgar Square commemorates Admiral Horatio Nelson's defeat of Napoleon's navy in 1805 at Cape Trafalgar, off the southern tip of Spain. Nelson himself stands nearly 6 metres high from tip to toe on a 51-metre column, guarded by the bronze lions of Sir Edwin Landseer, and shares his plinth with a thousand well-fed

Trafalgar Square

NATIONAL PORTRAIT GALLERY

pigeons peeping down on the visitors below, taking aim.

The start of the Christmas season is always marked by the raising of a giant tree in Trafalgar Square and at midnight on New Year's Eve too many people for the square to hold sway back and forth with 'Auld Lang Syne' to the chimes of Big Ben. More serious demonstrations have been held here since 1848 when a crowd 15,000 strong gathered to protest against income tax. The suffragettes gathered here too, some years later, and not so long ago anti-poll tax demonstrators continued the tradition. Nelson looks over their heads to the main streets of London: to the east, the Strand, one of the oldest roads in London, leading to the City and the Tower; to the south, Whitehall, from whose ministries Britain once ruled a quarter of the earth; to the west, the Mall and Buckingham Palace, official home of the Queen, flanked by the peaceful greenery of the royal parks.

National Gallery

FROM CONSTABLES TO KINGS

Behind the admiral sits the squat glory of the **National Gallery**, opened in 1838 by the young Queen Victoria. It contains over 2000 masterpieces, including Constable's *The Haywain*, and is visited by over 3 million people a year.

Its neighbour, the **National Portrait Gallery**, has portraits of the notable deceased on its upper floors and more modern portraits on the ground floor. Shakespeare sports a fashionable earring.

Outside, cross carefully past the memorial to Nurse Edith Cavell, a First World War martyr, to the church of **St Martin-in-the-Fields**. Once upon a time this really did

Trafalgar Square

ADMIRALTY ARCH

CARLTON HOUSE TERRACE

stand in the fields. It is the parish church of the Admiralty as well as being a regular concert venue. Nell Gwyn is buried here in the area where she plied her early trade (she sold more than oranges). There is a good cafe in the crypt, a brass rubbing centre and a small art gallery.

National Portrait Gallery

St Martin-in-the-Fields

HIGHWAY OF PAGEANTRY

A brisk 15-minute walk through Admiralty Arch along the pink-surfaced **Mall** leads to Buckingham Palace. But first, on the right is the rear of **Carlton House Terrace**, the starting point for a massive reconstruction of London prepared by architect John Nash for the Prince Regent (later George IV), who lived in Carlton House. Number 6 Carlton House Terrace is the home of the Royal Society, whose Fellows have always been the pioneers of science of every age since 1660, among them Newton, Faraday and Darwin. It was round the corner from here, in Pall Mall, that the first street gas lamps glowed as early as 1807.

On the left of the Mall is **St James's Park**, laid out on instructions from Charles II, who introduced the pelicans, whose descendants are still to be seen on the lake. The daffodils are spectacular in the spring. Just before arriving

ST JAMES'S
PARK

The Mall

ST JAMES'S
PALACE

BUCKINGHAM
PALACE

at Buckingham Palace, in Marlborough Road, is **St James's Palace**, a Tudor mansion built by Henry VIII and containing state apartments designed by Wren. The gatehouse has the initials of Henry and the ill-fated Anne Boleyn carved over the doors. Queen Victoria was married in the **Chapel Royal** whose choirboys still wear the Tudor scarlet and gold costume. Ambassadors to Britain are appointed to the Court of St James, a reminder that the palace was the monarch's residence until Queen Victoria chose to live at the big house at the end of the

road. Visitors are no longer permitted to visit the palace for security reasons though the chapel is sometimes open for Sunday services. The Queen Mother lives in nearby **Clarence House**. *St James's Park*

BUCKINGHAM PALACE

Buckingham Palace was started in 1703 for the Duke of Buckingham and was faced with its present Portland stone only in 1913. The Royal Standard flies from the flagpole when the Queen is in residence. The changing of the guard takes place on dry days at 11.30 every day in the summer and on alternate days in the winter. See Traditional events section for details. It is one of the great free shows of London, with bands playing and immaculate drills setting off the brilliance of the uniforms.

Art-lovers will find a detour to the **Queen's Gallery** rewarding. Keeping the palace on your right, follow the walls round the corner to Buckingham Palace Road. The gallery shows a small selection of the much larger collection owned by the Queen and the paintings are changed periodically to reflect different themes and artists.

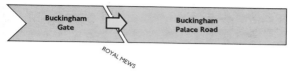

Buckingham
Gate

Buckingham
Palace Road

ROYAL MEWS

SLOWCOACHES

Keep the walls of the palace still on your right – they enclose a pretty landscaped country garden with sweeping trees and a lake which has made this something of a tiny nature reserve – until you reach a small door with a tiny notice announcing that this is the public entrance to the **Royal Mews**, open on two afternoons a week (three in summer and one in winter).

The mews houses the royal state coaches, of which the most opulent is the Gold State Coach first used by George III at the opening of Parliament in 1762 and now reserved for the Queen's use on grand occasions, when it is pulled by eight horses at walking pace. This is instantly recognisable as the model coach in all the souvenir shops. The open State Landau built for Edward VII is in regular use on state visits by foreign heads of government, and also on show is the Glass Coach, used by bride and groom at royal weddings. The royal cars are housed in another wing of the old stables and can sometimes be seen driving through the main yard. There are shops and pubs across the road for a lunch break.

Apsley House

NUMBER 1 LONDON

The best plan now is to catch any bus going to Hyde Park Corner. As you have a choice of several, the wait will be quite short. You need to cross Buckingham Palace Road to find the stop, keeping the palace garden wall on your right. Ask the conductor to tell you where to get off, or, as the bus swings right round the traffic hell of Hyde Park Corner, press the request stop button high up on the platform (or pull the wire running along the ceiling) just once. The bus goes past the door of **Apsley**

Buckingham Palace

House, once the home of the Duke of Wellington, but this cannot be approached overground as crossing Park Lane is impossible. There is a subway near the bus stop. Look on negotiating it as an initiative test.

Unlike Nelson, who died in his hour of triumph, the victor of Waterloo lived many years to become a tough, revered and feted prime minister. When Crystal Palace, the home of the Great Exhibition in 1851, became plagued with sparrows, the story goes that Queen Victoria called in the great military strategist to solve the problem, which he did with the terse reply: 'Sparrowhawks, Ma'am'.

Apsley House is now a museum, a handsome building by Robert Adam adjoining the Decimus Burton screen at Hyde Park Corner. It was called Number 1 London as it was the first house passed by coaches entering London through the Knightsbridge toll gate. Wellington had additions made to the house, including the Waterloo Gallery, formerly the setting of the annual dinner commemorating England's final victory over Napoleon in a field near a Belgian village in 1815.

The security guard will politely search your bags. This is quite common all over London now and just has to be endured, for safety's sake. Hyde Park tube station is back down the subway if you wish to break here for today. If not, and you feel like food, there are places to eat around Piccadilly. My favourite restaurant, L'Artiste Musclé, is in **Shepherd Market**, a quiet pedestrianised area with antique shops and floral hanging baskets, though it has a £7 minimum charge at lunchtimes to discourage the poor.

HYDE PARK

And back down the Hyde Park subway again. Pop up on the south side of Knightsbridge and window-shop down the street towards Harrods. Across the road, where Hyde

HARRODS

Brompton Road

BROMPTON ORATORY

Park shades into buildings and the Hyde Park Hotel, the brown track of **Rotten Row** can just be discerned. This was the *Route du Roi*, where Beau Brummell and the Regency beau monde went for a gallop. Brummell would be dressed completely in black, a fashion he set for gentlemen at around the same time that swords went out and umbrellas came in, much to Wellington's disgust: 'The Guards may in uniform, when on duty at St James's, carry them if they please; but in the field it is not only ridiculous but unmilitary.'

The Household Cavalry ride through Hyde Park from their barracks to Buckingham Palace every day at 10.30. Bicycling, however, is not allowed in the royal parks, though many cyclists break the rules.

KENSINGTON GORE

Just around here, almost opposite Sloane Street, is roughly the site of the bridge over the River Westbourne where two knights fought to the death in the Middle Ages – hence 'Knightsbridge'. The river still flows under the street from the Serpentine to its outlet in the Thames.

KENSINGTON STORE

Harrods

Bear left down Brompton Road and the familiar sight of **Harrods** invites a detour. A little further down Brompton Road are the boutiques and restaurants of fashionable Beauchamp Place. The white church across the road is **Brompton Oratory**, the leading Catholic church in London until Westminster Cathedral was finished in 1903.

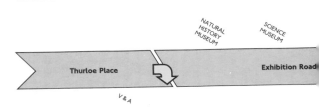

NATURAL HISTORY MUSEUM

SCIENCE MUSEUM

Thurloe Place

Exhibition Road

V & A

CULTURE CORNER

Almost next door is the **Victoria and Albert Museum**, and round the corner, the **Science**, **Natural History** and **Geological Museums**. There are seven miles of galleries in the V&A alone, covering thirteen acres, and to do all

A V&A exhibit

the museums justice takes at least a week. There might just be time to take in a free guided tour of the V&A, which takes an hour. Wait for the guide in the area under the dome just inside the main entrance. Excellent refreshments are obtainable at the museum.

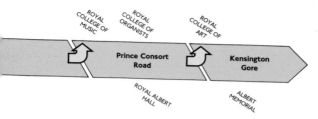

THE SOUND OF MUSIC

Walk north up Exhibition Road for a couple of minutes and turn left down Prince Consort Road as far as the **Royal College of Music**, which has a fascinating display of nearly 500 musical instruments as well as a collection of portraits. Its museum is primarily a place of study but visitors may be taken round on Wednesday afternoons in term time. The entrance is a bit off-putting as all visitors are asked to report to the reception desk.

Across the road up the steps is the **Royal Albert Hall**, built out of the proceeds of the Great Exhibition, as were the South Kensington museums. It is best known as the venue for the summer Promenade Concerts. The terracotta on the outside was repaired in 1990 at a cost of £1 million and for the 1990s it is planned to restore the interior to its original splendour and to open up the hall for a greater variety of events, especially during the day. People who find steps difficult should return to Exhibition Road and walk round the corner.

The ornate building to your left was the **Royal College of Organists** for many years and next to it stands the **Royal College of Art**, which holds exhibitions.

PRINCE ALBERT

Across Kensington Gore the **Albert Memorial** commemorates the Prince Consort who did so much to improve the minds – and conditions – of the Victorians before he died of typhoid fever in 1861, ten years after the Great Exhibition that he had sponsored.

The exhibition, of Victorian achievements in arts, science and technology, was held in the Crystal Palace, erected in Hyde Park just east of the memorial, which was itself the height of Victorian engineering technology. It was designed by Joseph Paxton and was three times the

OVERLEAF: Royal Albert Hall

Kensington Gore

Kensington High Street

KENSINGTON HIGH STREET

KENSINGTON GARDENS

KENSINGTON PALACE

length of St Paul's Cathedral. It was later moved to a permanent site in Sydenham and burnt down in a spectacular fire in 1936. Albert himself, under his elaborate canopy, may still be trapped in a silver web of scaffolding, for restoration work.

KENSINGTON GARDENS

Now stroll into the park past the memorial and go westwards into **Kensington Gardens**, apparently a more formal extension of Hyde Park, but in fact the former gardens of **Kensington Palace**. The gardens are closed to the public at dusk, so don't try to outstay your welcome. It was here that the young Victoria was roused from her

Kensington Palace

bed to hear that she was Queen. Follow signposts to the Round Pond. (Note clean park toilets on the left.) The palace is the London home of the Prince of Wales and family, and Princess Margaret has apartments here, as do Prince and Princess Michael of Kent and the Gloucesters.

Bayswater Road

Some state apartments are open to the public, including the young Queen's bedroom where she held her Accession Council on the morning of 20 June 1837. On the floor below is displayed the Court Dress Collection from Victoria's reign to the 1950s. The Orangery may be open for a polite tea on rickety chairs.

A SERPENTINE RAMBLE

Kensington High Street tube station is not far away if you wish to end the tour here. Otherwise, head back across the gardens looking for the statue of **Peter Pan** by the Serpentine. Follow the path with the lake to your right and make your way through the northern part of Hyde Park towards Marble Arch. Be careful at the Victoria Gate. This is not the corner of the park that it seems. To the left is the Bayswater Road, but directly ahead a road full of traffic is allowed through the park itself. Keep Bayswater Road immediately to your left and walk alongside this park road for ten minutes for **Marble Arch**.

TYBURN TREE

The arch was designed by Nash to be the entrance to Buckingham Palace and was moved when it was found to be too narrow to admit the Queen's state coach. Today it is the centrepiece for an elaborate traffic island with a grisly past. Here at the crossroads, from the twelfth century to 1783, were hanged the villains and petty criminals of London from the triple tree of Tyburn. The permanent gallows, erected in 1571, was not constructed like the traditional noose. It was a tripod, like the frame of a giant three-legged table. The beams, perhaps 3 to 4 metres high, made a triangle in the air which could accommodate twenty-four ropes, eight for each beam. Hogarth's picture, *The Idle Apprentice Executed at Tyburn*, shows that there were stands erected nearby for spectators.

```
┌──────────────┬─────────┬──────────┬─────────────────────┐
│  Marble      │   ⊖     │   ⇨      │  Oxford Street      │
│  Arch        │         │          │                     │
└──────────────┴─────────┴──────────┴─────────────────────┘
 SPEAKERS'        MARBLE
 CORNER           ARCH
```

Where **Speakers Corner** is situated now was the grassy place 'where soldiers are shot' according to a map of 1746. Today the crowds still head here, especially on Sundays, to hear anyone who wishes to have their say. Oxford Street, the home of high street stores, once echoed to the shouts and jeers of the populace as those about to die were brought along 'Tyburn Road', as it used to be called, from Newgate Gaol on carts or hurdles.

Northwards lies Edgware Road, one of the most ancient roads in Britain. Later known as Watling Street, it was possibly constructed over a Celtic track by the Romans in the first century AD. To the south lies Park Lane, once the rural 'Tyburn Lane', but now a dual carriageway leading past the big hotels to Hyde Park Corner. To the west lie Bayswater and Notting Hill. The way to Marble Arch tube station is via another menacing ill-lit subway, for which the one at Hyde Park Corner was the training ground. If you want to continue directly to the next tour take the Central line tube directly to Chancery Lane; or take a number 8 bus along Oxford Street, then via New Oxford Street (where Dr Crippen had consulting rooms in 1910) and High Holborn to Chancery Lane tube station. The conductor will put you off at the right stop.

If you are travelling to London around Christmas and the New Year, please note that most major attractions are closed. A few places are closed on Mondays. Most places in the City are closed on Saturdays and Sundays.

D Attractions with this logo make an effort to welcome the disabled. Other places are accessible with help. Phone for details. See also Disabled in London section. Popular attractions have a queuing system for telephone callers. You lose your place in the queue by re-dialling, so stay on the line.

National Gallery, Trafalgar Square, WC2
071-839 3321
Free. Mon-Sat 10-6, Sun 2-6
U BR Charing Cross
Buses 1, 3, 6, 9, 11, 12, 13, 15, 15B, X15, 24, 29, 53, 53X, 77, 77A, 88, 109, 159, 170, 176, 177Ex, 184, 196
D Orange Street entrance

National Portrait Gallery, 2 St Martin's Place, WC2
071-306 0055
Free. Mon-Fri 10-5, Sat 10-6, Sun 2-6
U BR Charing Cross
Buses as National Gallery

St Martin-in-the-Fields, Trafalgar Square, WC2
Box office 071-839 1930
U BR Charing Cross
Buses as National Gallery
D Phone

Queen's Gallery, Buckingham Palace Road, SW1
071-930 4832, Recorded information 071-799 2331
Adults £2.00, Senior citizens £1.50, Children £1.00
Tue-Sat 10-5, Sun 2-5 (last admissions 4.30);
closed Mon except Bank Holidays
No toilets
U St James's Park, Victoria
Buses (to Victoria station) 2, 2A, 2B, 11, 16, 24, 25, 29, 36, 36A, 36B, 38, 39, 52, 52A, 73, 76, 82, 135, 177Ex, 185, 507, 510, C1

Royal Mews, Buckingham Palace Road, SW1
071-930 4832, Recorded information 071-799 2331
Adults £1.30, Senior citizens £1.00, Under 16 70p
Wed & Thur 12-4 (Wed, Thurs & Fri in summer; Wed only
in winter) except during Ascot; phone line gives full details
U St James's Park, Victoria
Buses as Queen's Gallery
D Phone, free

Apsley House, Hyde Park Corner, W1
071-499 5676
Adults £2.00, 5-15 & Concessions £1.00
Tue-Sun 11-5 (last admissions 16.30); closed Mon except
Bank Holidays
U Hyde Park Corner
Buses 2A, 2B, 9, 10, 14, 16, 19, 22, 25, 30, 36, 36B, 38,
52, 52A, 73, 74, 82, 135, 137, 503

Victoria and Albert Museum, Cromwell Road, SW7
071-938 8500, Recorded information 071-938 8441
Donations Adults £3.00, Children & Concessions 50p
Mon-Sat 10-5.50, Sun 2.30-5.50
U South Kensington
Buses 14, 30, 74, 503, C1
D

Science Museum, Exhibition Road, SW7
071-938 8000, Recorded information 071-938 5491
Adults £3.00, Senior citizens £2.00, Children & other
Concessions £1.75
Times as Natural History Museum
U South Kensington
Buses No buses run down Exhibition Road. Get off at V&A
and walk, or take 9, 10, 33, 52, 52A, C1 to Royal Albert
Hall (Queen's Gate)
D

Natural History Museum, Exhibition Road, SW7
Recorded information 042-692 7654
Adults £3.00, 5-18 & Concessions £1.50, Families (2+4) £8.00
Mon-Sat 10-6, Sun 1-6
Free. Mon-Fri 4.30-6, Sat, Sun & Bank Holidays 5-6
U South Kensington
Buses as Science Museum
D

Geological Museum, now incorporated with Science Museum

Royal College of Music, Museum of Instruments, Prince Consort Road, SW7
071-589 3643
Adults £1.20, Children & Concessions £1.00
Wednesdays in term time 2-4
U South Kensington
Buses as Science Museum
D Phone

Royal Albert Hall, SW7
Box office 071-589 8212
U South Kensington
Buses 9, 10, 33, 52, 52A, C1
D Phone

Royal College of Art, Kensington Gore, SW7
071-584 5020
Free. Mon-Fri 10-6
U High Street Kensington, South Kensington
Buses as Royal Albert Hall
D Access, toilet

Kensington Palace, W8
071-937 9561
Adults £3.75, Children £2.50, Concessions £2.80, Families (2+2) £11.00
Mon-Sat 9-5, Sun 1-5 (last admissions 4.15)
U Queensway, High Street Kensington
Buses 9, 10, 33, 49, 52, 52A, C1 to Palace Gate, Kensington Road
D Phone

The Queen's Gallery

Buckingham Palace

The Queen's Gallery was opened in 1962 to hold exhibitions based on the Royal Collection, one of the finest private art collections in the world.

CARLTON HOUSE
The Past Glories of George IV's Palace
22nd March, 1991-11th January, 1992

Described as 'Mahomet's paradise', Carlton House was the London residence of George IV who lavished vast sums on its decoration filling its rooms with works of art of outstanding quality and beauty.

Carlton House was demolished in 1827 and this exhibition brings together, for the first time, an unrivalled selection of the finest paintings and works of art from this former royal residence.

The Royal Mews

The Royal Mews at Buckingham Palace is a working stables where the state carriages and coaches, together with their horses and equipage, are housed.

For further information and opening arrangements for The Queen's Gallery and The Royal Mews, Buckingham Palace, contact your nearest Tourist Information Office or telephone 071 799 2331

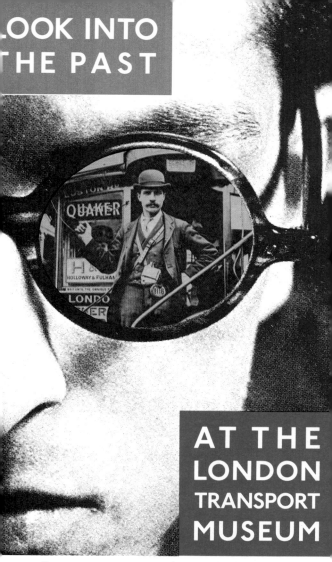

LOOK INTO THE PAST

AT THE LONDON TRANSPORT MUSEUM

Browse among our unique collection of historic vehicles, posters and archive film.

Put yourself in the driving seat of a London bus Underground train.

Visit the Museum Shop for the best selection of reproduction posters in town.

Open Daily 10.00-18.00. (Last admission 17.15). Museum closed 24/25/26 Dec. Phone 071-379 6344 071-836 8557 24 hr. information.

How to get there: *Underground:* Covent Garden or Leicester Square *British Rail:* Charing Cross. *Bus:* Any bus to Aldwych or Strand.

London Transport Museum, The Piazza, Covent Garden, London WC2E 7BB.

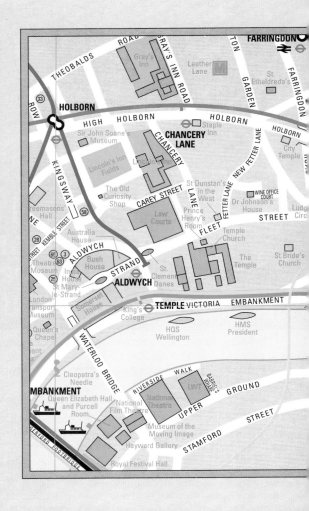

**LINCOLN'S INN
TEMPLE
FLEET STREET
ST PAUL'S
GUILDHALL
MUSEUM OF LONDON
BARBICAN**

WALK 2

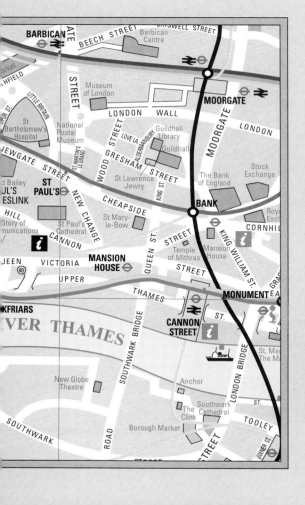

STAPLE INN

| High Holborn | Chancery Lane | Lincoln's Inn Fields |

CHANCERY LANE

LINCOLN'S INN

Near Chancery Lane tube station, on the south side of the street, is the Elizabethan building of **Staple Inn**, founded in 1378 as an Inn of Chancery. The old hall with its hammerbeam roof was destroyed in the war, like so much of this part of London, and has been restored. The modern façade in Holborn carefully matches its sixteenth-

century predecessor. The little dragon, or griffin, on its plinth set in the pavement outside the Inn marks the western boundary of the City of London. Saturday is a bad day to visit the City. The Temple, Inns of Court, rest-aurants and public conven-iences tend to be closed and everywhere is deserted. Make sure you do this walk during the week.

Staple Inn

LINCOLN'S INN

Turn down Chancery Lane and then right into the shady vaulted entrance to **Lincoln's Inn**. The Inn, as a company of lawyers, dates back in documents to 1422, by tradition even earlier, but the buildings are more modern. The

gateway from Chancery Lane is dated 1518. The Tudor-looking New Hall opposite has 1843 set in the brickwork. Former mem-bers of the Inn include Thomas More, John Donne, William Penn and President Eisenhower.

Lincoln's Inn

Across Lincoln's Inn Fields, a leafy London square, lived **Sir John Soane**, architect of the Bank of England. His house is now a museum, yet it is

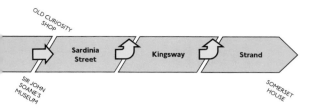

possible to imagine it as a lived-in pre-Victorian house, especially if you go down the quaint narrow passageways looking for the toilet.

Walking down towards Kingsway, the **Old Curiosity Shop** can be seen down Portsmouth Street, though one London historian points out that this was a heraldic sign-painter's shop when Dickens wrote his book. It sells old curiosities.

NO OIL PAINTING

Turn left down Kingsway – a dismal thoroughfare with nowhere to shelter from the rain. The subway in the middle used to be the old tramway tunnel to Waterloo Bridge. Facing up the street at the bottom is Bush House, at Aldwych, the home of the BBC World Service, with Australia House and the Indian High Commission nearby.

Sir John Soane's Museum

SOME OIL PAINTINGS

The **Courtauld Institute Galleries** at Somerset House are not far away in the Strand. Cross over the Strand to the south side, past King's College, go through the main archway of Somerset House and through a doorway on the right. The paintings are reached by a handsome but steep and slippery stone spiral staircase, or a little lift. The galleries are more informative than most, but some pictures reflect the lighting, which spoils them. The

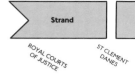

Impressionist and post-Impressionist paintings have pride of place.

THE BELLS PEAL

Turn right out of Somerset House, and see on your left Wren's church of **St Clement Danes**, the official church

St Clement Danes

St Dunstan-in-the-West

of the RAF – whose bells peal 'oranges and lemons' – towards the **Royal Courts of Justice**. A statue of Fleet Street's most famous resident, Samuel Johnson, has been erected at the far end of the church. Walking now down Fleet Street, notice the larger version of Holborn's little griffin marking the boundary of the City of London where Wren's **Temple Bar** used to stand. This arched gateway was moved to the country in 1888 because it was holding up the traffic. Wynken de Worde, Caxton's apprentice and heir, brought printing to Fleet Street from Westminster in around 1500 to premises near here. **St Dunstan-in-the-West**, on the left, is spiritually one of the oldest churches in the City, probably founded in the eleventh century, but it was rebuilt in 1832.

Fleet Street

'DREADFUL GOINGS ON'

Near here, it is said, worked Sweeney Todd, the Demon Barber of Fleet Street, providing the filling for Mrs Lovett's meat pies next door. On investigation Todd turns out to be the villain of a completely fictional story called 'The String of Pearls', first published in Fleet Street in 1846. It passed into Victorian melodrama, then folklore, and now the musical sings of the 'dreadful goings on going on'.

THE TEMPLE

The **Temple** takes its name from the Knights Templars of Jerusalem who established themselves as a wealthy mon-astic order in this area in the twelfth century. The much restored round **Temple church** was consecrated in 1185. It was modelled on the church of the Holy Sepulchre in Jerusalem. The order was dissolved in 1312 by the Pope after allegations of her-

Temple church

esy, and the land was given to the Knights Hospitallers, who leased much of it to the lawyers.

Middle Temple Hall was where a law student noted in his diary that Shakespeare's own company performed 'Twelfth Night' on 2 February 1602, and the elegant **Temple Gardens** were where, according to the great dramatist, York and Lancaster picked their white and red roses. The Temple suffered serious damage in the war.

JOHNSON'S FLEET STREET

At the foot of Chancery Lane, Number 17 Fleet Street, **Prince Henry's Room**, was once a seventeenth-century tavern called the Prince's Arms. Then it became The Fountain at the rear of the building, while from 1795 to

Fleet Street

Ludgate
Circus

ST BRIDE'S
CHURCH

1816 Mrs Salmon's waxworks were shown at the front. Mrs Salmon made the earlier waxworks herself and died in 1760 aged 90. Madame Tussaud, curiously, had a similar history a century later. The waxworks made Fleet Street famous many years before the newspaper business moved here. There is also an exhibition at Prince Henry's Room commemorating Samuel Pepys, who was born off Fleet Street in Salisbury Court in 1633.

The **Old Cock Tavern**, dated 1549, is not the Old Cock Tavern at all. The original was obliged to move house in 1887 to make way for a bank so they set up house nearer Temple Bar with as many of the old fixtures and fittings as they could take with them. The pub suffered a devastating fire in the winter of 1989-90. Johnson had frequented the old Old Cock, and his chair from the tavern rests empty at his house in Gough Square where he lived in the 1750s when he was compiling his famous dictionary. He used the garret running along the length of the top floor for his work, and had it fitted out with a long desk, where his clerks would write standing. This is yet another restored building.

Johnson is said also to have frequented the **Cheshire Cheese**, an ancient eating house hidden down a tiny alley, though he and Boswell had for regular haunts the Mitre, now only a plaque on a bank's wall, and Clifton's Chophouse, Butcher Row, roughly where the Royal Courts of Justice stand. The Cheshire Cheese is a victim of its own popularity and finds it difficult to cope with visitors who crowd in the tiny entrance, blocking the way for customers of the restaurant upstairs.

Behind the street towards the river there was once a Carmelite monastery (Whitefriars) near Bridewell Palace. The palace became the notorious Bridewell House of Correction for Women, one of the first prisons to introduce the treadmill. It was pulled down in 1863. All that

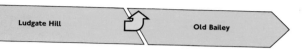

| Ludgate Hill | | Old Bailey |

remains of the monastery are the (private) wine cellars of the Cheshire Cheese.

PHOENIX FROM THE ASHES

St Bride's church rose like a phoenix from the ashes after the Great Fire of London, and had to be restored again after Hitler. The Press Association building jammed up against the church spoils the view of it more than somewhat – though it always was impossible to see it from any distance away except for a brief period in 1824 when yet another fire swept away the buildings shielding it from Fleet Street. The church is a must: the crypt contains a potted history of the church and the street from Roman times. It is said that the traditional tiered wedding cake was originally copied from the spire of St Bride's by an enterprising local baker.

St Bride's

THE DEVIL YOU KNOW

Crossing over Ludgate Circus to go up Old Bailey, think of the Fleet River coursing beneath your feet to run into the Thames under Blackfriars railway bridge. In the Middle Ages ten or twelve ships laden with merchandise could

| Old Bailey | → | Giltspur Street | ↘ |

CENTRAL CRIMINAL COURTS   BARTHOLOMEW'S ST HOSPITAL

sail side by side up the Fleet (now Farringdon Street) as far as Holborn, but so much filth was poured into it that it became a sewer and was eventually covered over. The English must prefer their familiar smells, however noxious, to the new and strange ...

... at the circus once stood the Rainbow Coffee House, opened in 1656. Just before Christmas 1657 the neighbours complained of the smell of coffee and the owner was charged with creating a nuisance.

SINNERS AND SAINTS

Most of the **Central Criminal Courts** in Old Bailey is modern. If you want to see where Crippen was tried, in Number 1 Court, the entrance is at the top of the street; turn right to join the queue for the small public gallery. The courts were built on the site of Newgate Prison, the scene of executions after the processions to Tyburn were stopped in 1783.

North of Old Bailey, via Giltspur Street, is **St Bartholomew's Hospital** – Bart's – founded in 1123 by the monk Rahere. As you approach Smithfield meat market at the top of Giltspur Street you should see to your right a half-timbered gatehouse which leads to the priory church of **St Bartholomew the Great** founded by Rahere at about the same time. Rahere's tomb is here. Amazingly the church not only survived the Fire of London but also the Luftwaffe. However, it fell into disuse for over 200 years and parts of it were used as a stable, blacksmith's forge, storeroom and factory. Benjamin Franklin worked here when it was a printer's shop in 1724. It was only completely reclaimed by the Church in 1929.

ST PAUL'S

Coming out of the gateway, turn left down Little Britain towards **St Paul's Cathedral** past the **National Postal**

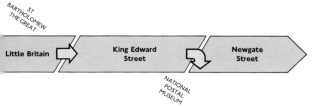

Museum with the Penny Black – the first adhesive stamp. The cathedral is approached by going through an office block and a barren grey square of rain-spattered concrete. Wren's tomb, in the crypt, reads (in Latin): 'If you seek his monument, look about you.' That noise must be Wren turning in his grave, or was it another skyscraper, edging even closer? The Prince of Wales, in his book, *Vision of Britain*, looks at the cathedral where he was married and despairs: 'Can you imagine the French doing

St Paul's Cathedral

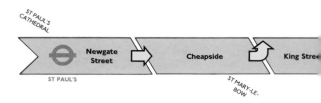

this sort of thing in Paris, on the banks of Seine around Notre Dame? ... When did we lose our sense of vision?'

Inside the cathedral it is possible to forget the damage that money can do and remember Wren's inscription. The serene beauty of the interior is gradually being eroded by the volume of visitors wearing out the fabric of the church and a donation is requested for its upkeep. For the ambulatory, crypt and galleries small charges are reluctantly made. The dome is not as big on the inside as it is on the outside, as it is in the form of a double skin. A doorway from the Whispering Gallery leads to an open staircase hanging in the black space between the two domes. It leads up for ever onto a narrow windy parapet overlooking London. Another doorway and another staircase lead down again. There are a lot of steps. Even more if you then descend to the crypt to view Wren's tomb. If you think we live longer in the twentieth century it comes as a shock to realise that Wren lived to be 91.

St Mary-le-Bow

If you wish to break the tour here, St Paul's tube station and bus stops are on the north side of the cathedral in Newgate Street. To continue, walk down the ancient thoroughfare of Cheapside as far as **St Mary-le-Bow**. Cockneys are only those born within the sound of Bow bells. As they called Dick Whittington back from as far away as Highgate to the City, that makes an awful lot of cockneys. In the fifteenth century a bell sounded at 9 in the evening for the apprentices to stop work for the day.

Aldermanbury | Love Lane | Wood Street | London Wall

GUILDHALL GUILDHALL LIBRARY CLOCKMAKERS· COMPANY MUSEUM MUSEUM OF LONDON BARBICAN

GUILDHALL

Turn up King Street, across the road, and cross Gresham Street to find **Guildhall**, home of the Corporation of the City of London. The building was completed in 1425, shortly after Whittington's death. Like so many buildings in the City, it suffered in the Great Fire and then the Blitz, fortunately losing only its roof each time. **The Guildhall Library**, founded by Whittington, is round the corner in Aldermanbury. It is a modern building, open to the public, which has a very small bookshop tucked out of sight with interesting reproduction maps and books on old London. **The Clockmakers' Company** has a small museum here open in office hours.

CONCRETE PALACE

The main goal for today is the **Museum of London**. From the Guildhall Library go down Love Lane opposite, turn right into Wood Street, then left into the modern highway of London Wall. The museum is across London Wall in the south-west corner of the Barbican. It is small compared with the British Museum or the South Kensington complex, but purpose designed so that visitors can immerse themselves in each period of London's history from prehistory to the twentieth century. Sir Mortimer Wheeler was director of the museum from 1926 to 1944. It was he who put the archaeology of London onto a sound basis, and the main work of the museum still is rescuing London's heritage from under the bulldozers. It's a very lively place with much of interest. Bits of the Roman wall are incorporated into the design of the museum and can be seen through the windows. There is a small cafe.

Leaving the museum and looking for either Barbican or Moorgate tube station, you may well stumble across the **Barbican Centre**, home of the London Symphony

London Wall

Orchestra and the Royal Shakespeare Company. There are places to eat and drink, shops and a library here, but the good earth is not beneath your feet.

To continue directly to the next tour take the Circle line via Liverpool Street from Barbican or Moorgate tube station to St James's Park. No change of trains is needed.

If you are travelling to London around Christmas and the New Year, please note that most major attractions are closed. A few places are closed on Mondays. Most places in the City are closed on Saturdays and Sundays.

D Attractions with this logo make an effort to welcome the disabled. Other places are accessible with help. Phone for details. See also Disabled in London section. Popular attractions have a queuing system for telephone callers. You lose your place in the queue by re-dialling, so stay on the line.

Sir John Soane's Museum, 13 Lincoln's Inn Fields, WC2
071-405 2107
Free. Tue-Sat 10-5
U Holborn
Buses 8, 17, 18, 22B, 25, 45, 46, 171A, 243, 259, 501 to Chancery Lane
D Phone

Courtauld Institute Galleries, Somerset House, WC2
071-872 0220
Adults £2.50, Under 16 & Concessions £1.00
Mon-Sat 10-6, Sun 2-6
U Temple
Buses 1, 4, 6, 9, 11, 13, 15, 15B, X15, 68, X68, 77, 77A, 168, 170, 171, 171A, 176, 177Ex, 188, 196, 501, 502, 505, 513 to Aldwych
D Phone

Prince Henry's Room, 17 Fleet Street, EC4
071-353 7323
Free. Mon-Fri 1.45-5, Sat 1.45-4.30
U Temple
Buses 4, 6, 9, 11, 15, 15B, X15, 171A, 502, 513

Dr Johnson's House, 17 Gough Square, Fleet Street, EC4
071-353 3745
Adults £1.50, Concessions £1.00
May to September Mon-Sat 11-5.30; October to April Mon-Sat 11-5
U Temple, Blackfriars
Buses as to Prince Henry's Room

Central Criminal Courts, Newgate Street and Old
Bailey, EC4
071-248 3277
U St Paul's

National Postal Museum, King Edward Street, EC1
071-239 5420
Free. Mon-Thur 9.30-4.30, Fri 9.30-4
U St Paul's
Buses as to St Paul's or Museum of London
D Phone

St Paul's Cathedral, EC4
071-248 2705
Donation Adults £1.00, Under 16 60p
Galleries Adults £2.70, Under 16 & Senior citizens £1.10,
Students £1.85
Crypt Adults £1.70, Under 16 70p, Students £1.15
Ambulatory Adults £1.00, Students 50p, Under 16 &
Senior citizens free
Galleries, crypt and ambulatory: Mon-Fri 10-4.15,
Sat 11-4.15
Sung Evensong 5 pm daily (not August when choir on
tour). The crypt may be closed for services.
Guided tours Adults £5.00, Under 16 & Senior citizens
£2.50, Students £4.00
Mon-Sat unless service 11 am, 11.30, 2 pm, 2.30
U St Paul's
Buses 4, 8, 22B, 25, 141, 501, 502
D Access to main body and crypt with helper

City Information Centre in St Paul's Churchyard
071-606 3030

Guildhall, off Gresham Street, EC2P 2EJ
Free to Great Hall daily 10-5 provided there is no function
on. Free tour by written application to The Keeper
includes Old Library and Crypt.
U Bank
Buses as to St Paul's and walk along Cheapside
D Limited but improving, phone

Clockmakers' Company Collection, Guildhall Library, EC2
071-606 3030
Free. Mon-Fri 9.30-5
U Bank
Buses as to St Paul's and walk along Cheapside
D Phone

Museum of London, London Wall, EC2
071-600 3699
Free. Tue-Sat 10-6, Sun 2-6 (last admissions 5.30);
closed Mon except Bank Holidays
U Barbican, St Paul's, Moorgate
Buses 4, 141, 279A, 502
D Phone 071-600 3699 ext 280 for details of road access
and parking

Barbican Centre, Silk Street, EC2
071-638 4141, Recorded information 071-628 9760,
Box office 071-638 8891
U Barbican, Moorgate
BR Moorgate
Buses as to Museum of London or 9, 11, 21, 43, 76, 141,
214 to Finsbury Square
D Parking, access

CABINET WAR ROOMS

VISIT THE
NERVE CENTRE
OF BRITAIN'S
WAR EFFORT

OPEN DAILY
⊖ WESTMINSTER

CLIVE STEPS, KING CHARLES STREET,
LONDON SW1A 2AQ 01-930 6961

Bank *of* England Museum
Bartholomew Lane EC2

Open Mon - Fri 10.00-17.00 all year.
Sun and Bank Hols 11.00-1700
from 29/3 to 29/9.

Admission Free
071 601 5545

WEST END TICKETS

14 CHARING CROSS ROAD, LONDON WC2

071 240 2337 10 lines
FAX 071 836 5049

WE OBTAIN THE UNOBTAINABLE TICKETS

"MISS SAIGON"
"ASPECTS OF LOVE"
"LES MISERABLES"
"CATS"
"PHANTOM OF THE OPERA"

AND ALL WEST END SHOWS

ALSO ALL SPORTING EVENTS
WIMBLEDON   F.A.CUP   CRICKET
HENLEY REGATTA   ROYAL ASCOT

ALL CONCERTS
WEMBLEY   HAMMERSMITH,
LONDON ARENA   ALBERT HALL

FREE DELIVERY THROUGHOUT CENTRAL LONDON

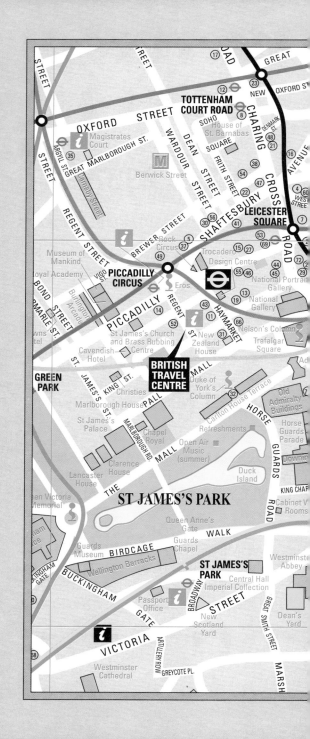

WALK 3

WESTMINSTER ABBEY
PARLIAMENT
DOWNING STREET
HORSE GUARDS
COVENT GARDEN
ROYAL OPERA HOUSE
PICCADILLY CIRCUS

NEW
SCOTLAND
YARD

Broadway   **Victoria Street**

ST JAMES'S
PARK

Emerging from **St James's Park** tube station the first building to note is the tube station itself, in the marbled basement of London Transport's headquarters at 55 Broadway. Almost opposite is new **New Scotland Yard**, from 1967 the home of the Metropolitan Police.

This houses the famous Black Museum, unfortunately not open to the public, now in a modern setting. Walk past Scotland Yard into Victoria Street. Down to your right is **Westminster Cathedral**, with its lift to the viewing tower. To your left is **Westminster Abbey**, recently restored by cleaning to a brilliant whiteness. It was originally consecrated to St Peter on 28 December

New *New Scotland Yard*

1065, though nothing of the pre-Norman abbey remains and much of the exterior, matching the Houses of Parliament, is nineteenth century.

IMMORTAL REMAINS

Edward the Confessor died eight days after the church was consecrated and was buried behind the altar. Since then every monarch has been crowned in the abbey except the uncrowned Edward V and Edward VIII. It has always been a burial place for monarchs, statesmen and politicians as well as literary and artistic giants. These are remembered in Poets' Corner, whose latest memorial is to Laurence Olivier. Here also are memorials, if not the mortal remains, of Chaucer, Ben Jonson (buried standing up), Shakespeare (modelling the £20-note here), Milton, Wordsworth, Keats and Shelley and, on a musical note,

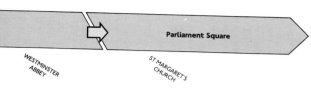

WESTMINSTER ABBEY

Parliament Square

ST MARGARET'S CHURCH

Handel and Vaughan Williams.

The oldest part of the abbey is the Norman undercroft of the Monks' Dormitory, built before 1100. Now a museum, it has a display of royal and other effigies, some modelled from death masks. The Duchess of Richmond (d.1702), who was quite a character, has her pet parrot beside her, believed to be the oldest stuffed bird in Europe. Its mistress was Charles II's favourite until he took a fancy to Nell Gwyn and in later life the ennobled courtesan was obliged to pay suitors for their services. (She can now be seen on the 50p coin as she modelled for Britannia.) Henry VII, modelled from his death mask, looks like a bank manager.

Westminster Abbey

ST MARGARET

From the abbey, visit the smaller church of **St Margaret** in the grounds. Dating from the late fifteenth century, this has been the official church of the House of Commons since 1614. It contains a memorial to William Caxton, the father of printing, and here is buried most of Sir Walter Raleigh. (His head is at West Horsley, Surrey.) Both Samuel Pepys and Sir Winston Churchill were married here. There are entrances at both ends of the church.

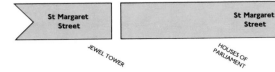

JEWEL TOWER

HOUSES OF PARLIAMENT

PALACE OF WESTMINSTER

Exit St Margaret's directly opposite the Houses of Parliament and turn right for a look at the **Jewel Tower**, a moated survival of the mediaeval palace, built in 1365. It

originally housed the personal treasure of Edward III and for two centuries was the record office of the House of Lords.

Across the road are the **Houses of Parliament**. When Parliament is in session the Union flag flies from the tower and a light shines in the clock tower above Big Ben. The old Westminster Palace, where Guy

Jewel Tower

Fawkes was left guarding kegs of gunpowder in 1605, was burned down in 1834. A competition to design a new one was won by Sir Charles Barry, whose creation has detailed work by Pugin. The Great Clock was raised in the summer of 1856 during celebrations of the victory in the Crimea. Its bell is said to have been named after the first Commissioner of Works, Sir Benjamin Hall. Its minute hands are each as tall as a double-decker bus.

Houses of Parliament

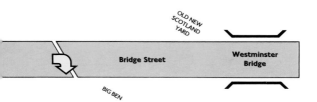

Big Ben

Although the public galleries are still open to the public, the buildings are not. It is possible to be invited by your MP or a peer but security is airport tight and guards will not permit baggage. Prior permission is required to visit Westminster Hall, which survived the fire. It was built by William Rufus in 1097 and rebuilt by Richard II in 1398. Under its hammerbeam roof Charles I stood accused in January 1649. It was originally part of the royal palace until Henry VIII moved to Whitehall Palace, now gone, in 1529 (see below).

WESTMINSTER BRIDGE

Walk towards Big Ben and turn right round the corner towards the river, past the statues of Richard the Lionheart and Oliver Cromwell. On the bridge, above the public conveniences, is Thornycroft's sculpture of the Queen of the Iceni, Boadicea, who led her people against the Roman City of London in the first century AD. She is said to be buried

Boadicea

under King's Cross station. The striped Norman Shaw building on the embankment is old **New Scotland Yard**, used from 1890 to 1967. This is the one seen in all the black and white thrillers set in fog-bound London.

Westminster Pier below is a convenient place to break

Bridge Street		Parliament Street

Old New Scotland Yard

the tour if you wish to catch a river boat downstream to the Tower, or upstream to Chelsea, Kew Gardens or Hampton Court (see Side trips). To continue, return to Westminster Pier, or Westminster tube station on the District and Circle lines. Eating places near here are rather expensive.

REMEMBERING THE WAR

In Whitehall, the **Cenotaph**, designed by Edwin Lutyens, stands as a memorial to the fallen of two world wars. It is here that the Queen and other members of the Royal Family lay wreaths on the second Sunday in November, followed by the Prime Minister and other national leaders.

In King Charles Street (to your left through the triple archway and down the steps at the far end of the street) are the **Cabinet War Rooms**, the underground suite of offices used by Churchill and the Cabinet during the Second World War. It was from Churchill's bedroom here that he made some of his most famous wartime speeches. The map room, with its coloured telephones, was manned constantly during the war to keep the Prime Minister and the King up to date with events. In the transatlantic telephone room was the telephone link with President Roosevelt, installed in 1943. The rooms were closed in 1945 and left untouched until preparations for visitors took place a few years ago. Included in the price of the ticket is a tape-recorded guide which re-creates the

DOWNING
STREET

Whitehall

CENOTAPH

wartime atmosphere in stereo. It is all excellently pro-
duced but there need to be more chairs. The one chair I
saw was being monopolised by a large determined lady.

DOWNING STREET

A little further down Whitehall is **Downing Street**, now
fenced off permanently as a security measure. The Prime
Minister's official residence is at Number 10 and the
Chancellor of the Exchequer lives at Number 11. An
earlier resident of Downing Street, in a house now
demolished, was James Boswell, Samuel Johnson's
biographer, who lodged here in 1762-63 while he was in
London trying to purchase a commission. The street was
built around 1680 by George Downing, a native of Mass-
achusetts and one of the earliest Harvard undergraduates,

Cabinet War Rooms

Whitehall

BANQUETING HOUSE

who became Secretary to the Treasury. Number 10 has been the official residence of the Prime Minister since Sir Robert Walpole lived there in 1732.

PALACE OF WHITEHALL

A few hundred yards on and you are at **Horse Guards**, the site of the old guard house to the former Palace of Whitehall, which is still guarded by mounted men from the Household Cavalry. The guard is changed daily at 11 o'clock, just preventing watching that and reaching Buckingham

The Banqueting House

Palace for their 11.30 changing of the guard. Behind, on Horse Guards Parade, formerly a tilting ground, the great Trooping the Colour ceremony takes place every year to celebrate the Queen's official birthday in June.

The **Banqueting House**, on the right, designed by Inigo Jones, was erected in 1625 as part of a plan to rebuild the palace until funds ran out. It was the Court of Charles I, who was executed in front of it in 1649. The

PREVIOUS PAGE: Horse Guards Parade

Strand **Villiers Street**

rest of the palace burned down in 1698 so William III took his Court to St James's Palace. The hall itself is on the first floor and takes only about a minute to view unless you are a serious art-lover.

OLD SCOTLAND YARD

As you walk towards Trafalgar Square note Great Scotland Yard on your right where both Inigo Jones and Wren lived. Number 4 Whitehall Place, the first headquarters of the Metropolitan Police, founded in 1829, had its back entrance and station house in Great Scotland Yard until 1890, and it was here, in 1884, that the Fenians planted a bomb in the urinal leaning against the building. Fortunately no one was hurt in the blast, though the windows of the Rising Sun pub opposite were blown in. The enterprising landlord charged threepence each to view the wreckage. Everything has been obliterated by progress, except the pub on the corner. I can't tell if it is the same one.

DOWN TO THE RIVER

Turn right at the statue of Charles I, along the Strand past the mainline Charing Cross station, and down Villiers Street towards the river, a reminder that once George Street, Villiers, Duke Street, Of Alley (now York Place) and Buckingham Street spelt out the name of the original landowner bit by

Embankment Gardens

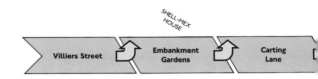

bit. It was here that the Adams brothers created the elegant Adelphi, with a river frontage based on the palace of the Roman Emperor Diocletian at Split, Yugoslavia.

Walk through Victoria Embankment Gardens as far as Shell-Mex House, formerly the Cecil Hotel (1886) and

Savoy theatre

Savoy Hotel

turn up towards the **Savoy theatre** and Hotel. The gas lamp by the cabstand is lit by gases rising from the sewers below. The **Savoy Hotel** was built by Richard D'Oyly Carte in 1884. He had also built the Savoy theatre as a home for Gilbert and Sullivan's comic operas. The name 'Savoy' comes from the Savoy Palace rebuilt as a hospital by Henry VII in 1510-16. Now only the private **Queen's Chapel** remains. It is open for services on Sundays at 11.

Covent Garden

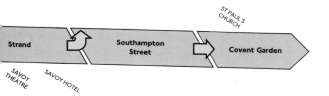

VEGETARIAN PIAZZA

Back in the Strand, once literally the river's shore, walk up Southampton Street and into **Covent Garden**. The Dukes of Bedford once owned an immense tract of land running from the river through Covent Garden to the elegance of the Bloomsbury squares in the north. Here was once the 'convent garden' of Westminster Abbey, though there was never an actual convent here. In the early seventeenth century Inigo Jones created an Italianate piazza here, though without the huge pillared building now in the centre, which became the power house of the nation's fruit, flower and vegetable market. Pressures of space and traffic forced the market to move out to Vauxhall in 1974, leaving the piazza for the enjoyment of the people, as its architect intended, and the central hall has become the home of smart shops, continental cafes and collectors' stalls.

THE OTHER ST PAUL'S

St Paul's church, the actors' church, at the west end of the piazza, was built in 1633 and was described by Jones as 'the handsomest barn in England'. The church faces away from the square into a quiet garden still lit by gas (possibly, like the Savoy, from the sewers)

St Paul's, the actors' church

and the elegant portico to the piazza backs onto the altar. It was under the portico that Shaw set the opening of 'Pygmalion' (later the musical 'My Fair Lady'), and it was here that Pepys watched the first Punch and Judy show.

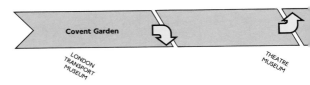

Covent Garden

LONDON TRANSPORT MUSEUM

THEATRE MUSEUM

Punch and Judy can still be seen here, or jugglers, or even a jester in cap and bells drinking from a Thermos flask, waiting his turn to take the floor.

INCONVENIENCES

Consequently the area attracts so many people that in the afternoons the public conveniences near the church are too few for the hordes of visitors.

REQUEST STOP

Across the piazza the Old Flower Market now houses the **London Transport Museum**, a fine collection of historic vehicles in a Victorian glasshouse, including an early 'knifeboard' horse bus where passengers sat back to back on the roof. You can also try the controls of a bus, and even a tube train. The excellent museum shop has reproductions and postcards of London Transport posters, a history of art in itself.

London Transport Museum

ROYAL OPERA HOUSE

Long Acre

BOSWELL AND JOHNSON

Turn right out of the museum and right again into Russell Street. Here at Number 8 is a coffee house on the site of the bookshop where Boswell met Dr Johnson on 16 May 1763. 'I drank tea at Davies's in Russell Street and about seven came in the great Mr Samuel Johnson, whom I have so long wished to see. As I knew his moral antipathy at the Scotch, I cried to Davies, "Don't tell him where I come from." However, he said "From Scotland." "Mr Johnson," said I, "indeed I come from Scotland, but I cannot help it." "Sir," replied he, "that, I find, is what a very great many of your countrymen cannot help."' The building is close to the **Theatre Museum**.

BOW STREET

Royal Opera House

Round the corner to the left, in Bow Street, the **Royal Opera House** today presents ballet and opera where once John Beard, the celebrated tenor and actor-manager, led his players. And here the Bow Street magistrates' police office operated from 1740, with its famous runners, the earliest London detectives, founded by novelist and magistrate Henry Fielding in 1753. The old magistrates' police office and court was across the road from the present imposing building but has been demolished. To the south rises the **Theatre Royal**, Drury Lane, once run by David Garrick, the actor-manager who came down to London with Samuel Johnson from Lichfield in 1737, both of them to make their fortunes. An earlier theatre on the site was re-opened after the

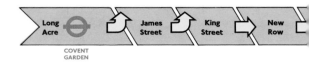

COVENT
GARDEN

restoration of the monarchy in the 1660s by Charles Hart,
actor-manager and great-nephew of William Shakespeare.
Pity no one remembers him. They remember his canny
teenage mistress better – Nell Gwyn.

Covent Garden tube station is not far away in James
Street if you wish to break here, or Leicester Square
station is only five minutes' walk if the Northern line is
more useful to you.

FAREWELL LEICESTER SQUARE

Walk back through the piazza (King Street) to New Row
and cross St Martin's Lane into theatreland. St Martin's
Court leads to Charing Cross Road and its many
bookshops, where you can cut through to **Leicester
Square**. Once the home of the Earl of Leicester, the
square became a sporting centre for boxing and billiards
before being absorbed into the neon glitter of London
nightlife. Shakespeare is in the centre, a copy of the £20-
note pose from Westminster Abbey.

PICCADILLY CIRCUS

Head quickly through Coventry Street to the old hub of
the British Empire, **Piccadilly Circus**. The statue of Eros
isn't Eros at all, but the Angel of Christian Charity, a
memorial to the philanthropic Seventh Earl of Shaftesbury.
The statue – an emblem of the epicentre of London – was
shifted a few feet not long ago and realigned, which
somehow seems as unthinkable as demolishing St Paul's
Cathedral on the grounds that it no longer fits in with the
surrounding architecture.

PICCADILLY

Step down Piccadilly as far as **Fortnum and Mason's** to
arrive opposite the shop on the hour. Mr Fortnum and Mr
Mason, who founded the shop in 1707, are modelled on

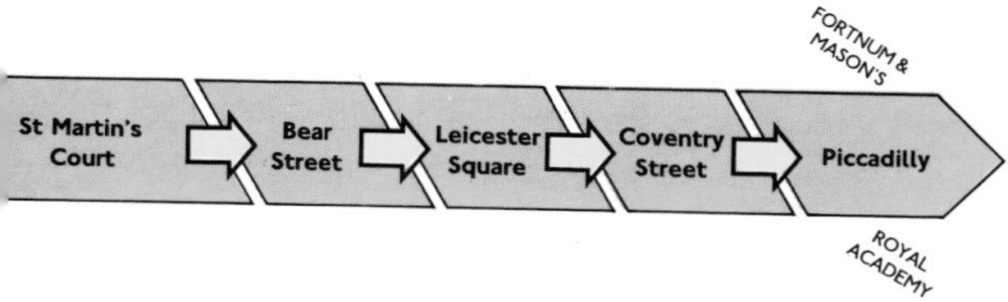

St Martin's Court → Bear Street → Leicester Square → Coventry Street → Piccadilly

FORTNUM & MASON'S

ROYAL ACADEMY

the clock above and bow to each other on the chime. The **Royal Academy**, on the north side of the street in Burlington House, holds the Summer Exhibition in July and is well worth a detour. Anyone can submit a picture for the exhibition and I believe the panel choose the best of amateur and professional artists anonymously.

Burlington Arcade, a little further on, was built in 1819 and is lined with attractive shops. A notice forbids singing, whistling or hurrying. The **Museum of Mankind** is at the rear of Burlington House. Winding your way back to Piccadilly Circus via Vigo Street and Regent Street, peep into the **Café Royal**. Once the haunt of Oscar Wilde and the Edwardian trendsetters, it still boasts fine food and wines as its Forte.

To connect up to Walk 4 take the Piccadilly line from Piccadilly Circus going east and change at Holborn to the Central line for Bank.

If you are travelling to London around Christmas and the New Year, please note that most major attractions are closed. A few places are closed on Mondays. Most places in the City are closed on Saturdays and Sundays.

D Attractions with this logo make an effort to welcome the disabled. Other places are accessible with help. Phone for details. See also Disabled in London section. Popular attractions have a queuing system for telephone callers. You lose your place in the queue by re-dialling, so stay on the line.

St Edward's Tower, Westminster Cathedral, Victoria Street, SW1
071-834 7452
Adults 70p, Children & Concessions 30p
April to October daily 9.30-5
U St James's Park
Buses (to Victoria station) 2, 2A, 2B, 11, 16, 24, 25, 29, 36, 36A, 36B, 38, 39, 52, 52A, 73, 76, 82, 135, 177Ex, 185, 507, 510, C1
D Separate entrance to lift

Westminster Abbey, SW1
071-222 5152, Super Tours 071-222 7110
Super Tour (all of the below) £6.00 at regular intervals
Nave: Free. Mon-Sat 8-6 plus later opening Wed to 7.45, Sun between services except for worshippers
Royal Chapels, Poets' Corner: Adults £3.00, Under 16 60p, Concessions £1.50, With sound guide £4.00
Pyx Chamber, Chapter House, Undercroft Museum: Adults £1.60, Under 16 40p, Concessions 80p
Mon-Fri 9-4.45 (last admissions at 4), Sat 9-2.45 (last admissions at 2) and 3.45-5.45 (last admissions at 5), Wed 6-7.45 free entrance to all abbey
U Westminster
Buses 3, 11, 12, 24, 29, 53, 53X, 77, 77A, 88, 109, 159, 170, 177Ex, 184, 196, C1
D

Houses of Parliament, SW1

071-219 3000

Free. Open when Houses are in session

Visitors' Gallery House of Commons: Mon-Thur 2.30-10 or later, Fri 9.30-3

Visitors' Gallery House of Lords: Mon-Thur 3 to end of debating, Fri 11 to end of debating. Long queues, no baggage

U Westminster

Buses as to Westminster Abbey

D Phone

Other areas via your MP

Cabinet War Rooms, Clive Steps, King Charles Street, SW1

071-930 6961/ 071-416 5000

Adults £3.60, 5-16 £1.80, Concessions £2.70, Families (2+2 or more) are offered free admission for one child

Taped guides in English, French, German, Italian, Spanish and Japanese

Daily 10-6 (last admissions 5.15)

U Westminster

Buses 3, 11, 12, 24, 29, 53, 53X, 77, 77A, 88, 109, 159, 170, 177Ex, 184, 196

D

Banqueting House, Whitehall, SW1

071-930 4179

Adults £2.00, Children £1.35, Concessions £1.50

Mon-Sat 10-5 (last admissions 4.30)

U Westminster, Charing Cross

BR Charing Cross

Buses as to Cabinet War Rooms

London Transport Museum, Covent Garden, WC2

071-379 6344, Recorded information 071-836 8557

Adults £3.00, 5-16 & Concessions £1.50, Families (2+2) £7.00

Daily 10-6 (last admissions 5.15)

U Covent Garden

Buses (along the Strand) 1, 6, 9, 11, 13, 15, 15B, X15, 77, 77A, 170, 176, 177Ex, 196; (down Charing Cross Road) 24, 29, 176

D Free

Theatre Museum, Russell Street, WC2
071-836 7891
Adults £2.50, Children & Concessions £1.50
Tue-Sun 11-7 (last admissions 6.30)
U Covent Garden
Buses as for London Transport Museum
D

Royal Academy of Arts, Burlington House, Piccadilly, W1
071-439 7438, Recorded information 071-439 4996/7
Admission charges vary
Daily 10-6
U Green Park, Piccadilly Circus
Buses 9, 14, 19, 22, 38
D Phone

Museum of Mankind, 6 Burlington Gardens, W1
071-437 2224
Free. Mon-Sat 10-5, Sun 2.30-6
U Green Park, Piccadilly Circus
Buses 9, 14, 19, 22, 38
D Phone

BANK OF ENGLAND
MANSION HOUSE
WREN'S CHURCHES
MONUMENT
LONDON BRIDGE
TOWER
TOWER BRIDGE

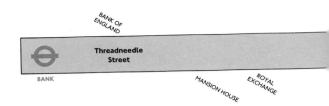

(NB: Saturday is a bad day to visit the City as many of its attractions are closed.)

The **Bank of England** stands at the heart of the City, at a point where seven major roads radiate in all directions. If you started out by trying to find the right steps up from Bank tube station's circular subway you may know this already. The bank – the Old Lady of Threadneedle Street – was founded in 1694 to lend money to the government for the war in France and moved to this site forty years later, though it has been rebuilt since. The vast curtain walls are now all that remain of Sir John Soane's bank, finished in 1833. The present building was completed just before the outbreak of war in 1939.

The **Bank of England Museum**, set within the walls, reconstructs John Soane's Bank Stock Office from 1793, faithfully carried out from his drawings. Security is strict, of course, because the museum has real gold on display, and is provided by the bank's security force. But don't let this put you off as they are very friendly and the museum is unique. I was quite astonished to learn that Kenneth Grahame, author of *The Wind in the Willows*, was secretary of the bank from 1898 to 1908. (He remained faithful to his beloved Thames, though, and used to take a river boat to work from his town house at Chelsea.)

CITY AT WORK

Next door, on the corner of Throgmorton Street, is the **Stock Exchange**. It had a viewing gallery until July 1990, when it was bombed by the IRA. Across the road from the bank is **Mansion House**, the palatial eighteenth-century home of the lord mayors of London and not at all near Mansion House tube station. It is here that the Lord Mayor, flanked by a fierce personal escort of pikemen and musketeers, receives his guests for great City banquets in

STOCK
EXCHANGE

the Egyptian Hall. The Mansion House is opened twice a week by prior appointment (written application), but miscreants and lawbreakers get to see inside where law-abiding citizens do not as this is the City's magistrates' court. Between the two buildings is the **Royal Exchange**, with its Classical portico. Opened in 1844 as a meeting place for tradesmen and merchants, it is now the home of

Royal Exchange

LIFFE, London International Financial Futures Exchange. The City at work can be seen from the public gallery around weekday lunchtimes.

CITY CHURCHES

Dip down again into the Bank tube subway and emerge at the Walbrook exit for the church of **St Stephen Walbrook**, one of Wren's fifty-two churches, and one which he himself worshipped at. The interior has been sympathetically restored and is striking for its airy cream dome, the first erected in England, beneath which is a central stone altar by Henry Moore. The circular arrangement of the church gives more of a community, sharing,

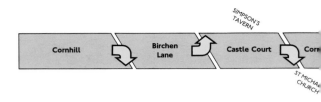

atmosphere than an authoritative altar with a raised pulpit. One gets the feeling that Christ would approve. This was the church where the Samaritans were founded by the rector in 1953. They continued to meet in the crypt until 1987 when Chad Varah retired from the service he started over a third of a century ago, though he remains rector.

Walk back the way you came towards Cornhill and turn right. Cornhill is one of the many streets which retain the names of the trades once found there. Others are Poultry, Shoe Lane, Pudding Lane, Milk Street and Bread Street. Turn right at Birchen Lane, then immediately left into Castle Court to **Simpson's Tavern**, completely hidden from the street at 38½ Cornhill. Re-emerge at yet another Wren church, **St Michael's**, with its tower by Hawksmoor added in 1721. This church contains a decorative carved wooden pelican dating from 1775. Turn right into Cornhill and right again into St Peter's Alley for a cramped view of Wren's **St Peter's church**, which holds lunchtime recitals, and emerge into Gracechurch Street.

COFFEE BREAK

Across the street lies **Leadenhall Market**, which took its name from a fourteenth-century lead-roofed mansion that stood nearby. Even earlier it was the site of the Roman basilica and other administrative buildings. It is now a glass-roofed Victorian arcade of shops and cafes, a reminder of an age when buildings were created for human beings. And although it is undoubtedly a traditional London market, where Pepys bought a leg of beef for sixpence, there is something relaxing and Parisian about it.

Beyond the market, in Leadenhall Street, is the new **Lloyd's** building, starkly, darkly, grey against the sky. Lloyd was the owner of a coffee house in the City where

businessmen met to trade. I'd tell you more but the public gallery and exhibition were closed on the day I visited

until further notice, because of the bomb in the Stock Exchange. Named parties booking in advance are still welcome. The information office is on the lower level round the corner in Lime Street.

Make your way back to Gracechurch Street and head downhill for the **Monument**. Monument tube station is presently covered in a grey construction site. A great deal of the City is being reconstructed and most of the work is done on Saturdays when there is no traffic.

Lloyd's building

MONUMENT

The Monument is the monument raised after the Great Fire of 1666. Night after night the glare of the flames lit up the sky as the fire, which had started in a baker's shop in Pudding Lane, crackled through the mediaeval wooden city. Gunpowder from the dockyards was used to demolish buildings in its path, but to no avail. When it ended at Pie Corner four-fifths of the old city, including at least 80 churches and 13,000 dwellings, were gone. Today the Monument, capped with a gilded flaming urn, invites the stout of leg to climb its 311 steps to view the new London that

Monument

Monument
Street

Lower Thames

BILLINGSGATE
FISH MARKET

Christopher Wren put in place of the old. Fortunately the higgledy-piggledy street lines were kept, unlike Baron Hausmann's grand sweep of boulevards in Paris. The Monument is at Fish Street Hill. If you look down the hill, you might be able to imagine that this ancient street was the approach road to the first **London Bridge**, whose massive timber beams have been discovered at the foot of the hill, where they were put by the Romans.

FROST FAIR

There have been several London Bridges. The most famous one was the one that was 'falling down' in the old nursery rhyme, with its nineteen arches, shops and centre chapel. It was here that the ice floes jammed under the arches on Boxing Day 1739, freezing the Thames for miles. Londoners soon made the river the site of a huge fair which lasted nine weeks until the February thaw. There were merry-go-rounds, games of skittles and bowls, donkey races and hot potatoes, even an ox roasting.

In the 1830s a bridge with wider arches was built, which quickened the river's flow, so now the lower reaches of the Thames remain unfrozen even in the coldest winters. It was this bridge which was dismantled to span the largely dry river bed of Lake Havasu City, Arizona. Some say the purchaser thought he was buying Tower Bridge. The present London Bridge was erected in 1968 and is not worth making a detour for.

Now walk away from the Monument down Monument Street, passing Pudding Lane and across the road to your right is the old **Billingsgate Fish Market**, which moved out to Docklands in 1982. This handsome Victorian building is by Horace Jones, who designed Leadenhall Market, though a market has been held on the site since before the thirteenth century. The old fish market stands over an immense cold store which at one

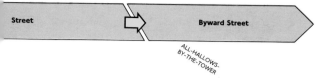

Street | Byward Street

ALL-HALLOWS-
BY-THE-TOWER

time solidified the foundations into a block of ice. Do not attempt to cross the dual carriageway as there is nothing more to be seen here.

SAMUEL PEEPS

Walk along the dual carriageway and follow the traffic as it bears left up Byward Street, and you will soon spot the greenish spire of **All Hallows-by-the-Tower**. The tiny balcony in the spire was where Samuel Pepys stood to survey the damage done by the Great Fire. The church can be reached via the subway. This is one of the most interesting and lively churches of the City and is well worth a detour. It has a small cafe, a museum in the crypt and a brass rubbing centre. All the City churches are desperate for money but some ask more nicely than others. A gift of £1 from every visitor per church would be acceptable.

All Hallows-by-the-Tower

TOWER HILL PAGEANT

The area between All Hallows and the Tower was bombed in the war – all that survived were the centuries-old cellars below, used in Victorian times for wine. The Tower Hill Pageant, in association with the Museum of London,

ST OLAVE'S

Seething Lane **Pepy's Street**

is planning to open London's first dark ride museum in these old vaults in the summer of 1991. In the lowest cellars of the vault, automated cars will take visitors in a 20-minute journey of the sights, sound and smells of London of the past 2000 years, through tableaux concentrating on the City and Port of London. The next floor up will have a display of the actual archaeological and historical finds, and the top floor (at ground level) will have speciality shops and restaurants. The lower levels will be reached by a scenic lift through the geological strata. This sounds as if it will be well worth checking out. Try *Time Out* or phone one of the numbers below for details of admission times and prices.

ST OLAVE

We owe so much of our knowledge of London during the time of the Great Fire to Pepys that it seems appropriate here to detour across the busy road for Seething Lane and the entrance to **St Olave's church** (note the skull-

St Olave's

decorated gateway). This was called by Pepys 'our own church' and here he and his wife are buried. Pepys worked in Seething Lane in the Navy Office. He and his friend Admiral Sir William Penn (whose son founded Pennsylvania) saved this church from the Great Fire by having the surrounding buildings torn down, but it was bombed in 1941 and, like so many, restored.

Trinity Square   Tower Hill

TOWER OF LONDON

TOWER HILL

Go along Pepys Street and turn down towards Trinity Square gardens, another execution site until the seventeenth century. Tower Hill tube station, like Monument, on the District and Circle lines, is close by if you wish to break the tour here. Traffic tears round Tower Hill and crossing the road would be suicidal but there is a subway and the Tower is signposted.

TOWER

William the Conqueror's Keep, the **White Tower**, started in 1078, remains the centrepiece of the later battlements and garrison buildings. It was white-washed from the time of Henry III (1216-72), hence its nickname. You enter the most visited attraction in London past the bearpits of the former Royal Menagerie (moved to Regent's Park Zoo in 1834). Not only was this once a royal zoo, but it has also been a prison (Rudolf

White Tower

Hess was one of the last prisoners for a short time in 1941), a royal palace, a mint and an observatory. It is still a royal treasury, housing the **Crown Jewels** in their thiefproof showcases. A new set of jewels had to be made for the coronation of Charles II in 1661, and presumably will one day be used to crown King Charles III. There is always a long queue.

When the river was used as one of London's principal highways, Traitor's Gate, leading up from the river, was

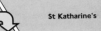

Minories   St Katharine's

the main entrance. For some it was a one-way trip. **Tower Green** was the site of the royal beheadings of Anne Boleyn and Catherine Howard, two of Henry VIII's wives, and Lady Jane Grey, Queen for nine days.

The young princes murdered in the Tower, the uncrowned Edward V and his younger brother, were not prisoners here. They lived and studied here while their mother and sisters lived a more social life in Westminster. Controversy still rages over whether Richard III (who reigned 1483-85) ordered their murder, but it seems unlikely as he had no motive. Their murder didn't make him next in line for the throne. The idea that Richard ordered his nephews' death was a Tudor rumour picked up by Shakespeare. The murder – whoever ordered it –

Beefeater

certainly happened, and gave the **Bloody Tower** its name. A later prisoner there was Sir Walter Raleigh, who spent several years here writing the *History of the World* after plotting against James I. And Guy Fawkes and his fellow conspirators went to the Tower for questioning after the Gunpowder Plot, though they were taken back to Westminster for execution.

The most colourful aspect of the Tower is the presence of the Yeoman Warders, or Beefeaters, founded in 1485 by Henry VII. Unlike the Guardsmen on sentry duty in Westminster, the Beefeaters are allowed to talk to visitors and in fact act as guides. The **Armouries** have the armour of Henry VIII as the main attraction.

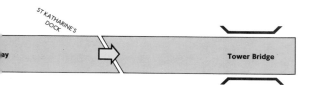

TOWER BRIDGE

Follow directions along the walkway for **Tower Bridge** and the ticket office at the base of the north tower. Both towers have exhibitions and on the south side the old machinery can be viewed. London's best-known landmark

is a masterpiece of Victorian engineering, half cantilever and half suspension bridge. It cost more than £1 million in 1894.

Returning to the north side of the river, follow directions to **St Katharine's Dock**, with its quaint shops and marina of tall ships and cruisers. The old *Nore* lightship is moored here, near the Dickens pub, which needs no extra advertising and is set in a new quayside apartment complex designed in Instant Picturesque. The advantage of this style of architecture is that, like

Tower Bridge

old silver, it will become more beautiful with time.

Now return to Tower Hill tube station, or the Docklands Light Railway at Tower Gateway if you wish to explore further east. To connect up to Walk 1, take any tube going west to Embankment and walk up the hill to Charing Cross and Trafalgar Square.

St Katharine's Dock

If you are travelling to London around Christmas and the New Year, please note that most major attractions are closed. A few places are closed on Mondays. Most places in the City are closed on Saturdays and Sundays.

D Attractions with this logo make an effort to welcome the disabled. Other places are accessible with help. Phone for details. See also Disabled in London section. Popular attractions have a queuing system for telephone callers. You lose your place in the queue by re-dialling, so stay on the line.

Bank of England Museum, EC2
071-601 5793
Free. Mon-Fri 10-5
U Bank
Buses 6, 8, 9, 11, 15B, X15, 21, 22B, 25, 43, 76, 133, 149, 214, 501 to Bank
D Phone

Stock Exchange, Old Broad Street, EC2
071-588 2355, ext 29770
Closed. Phone for latest information.
U Bank
Buses as for Bank Museum
D Phone

Mansion House, EC4N 8BH
Free. Tue-Thur 11-2 by written application to the Principal Assistant
U Bank
Buses as for Bank Museum

LIFFE, Royal Exchange, EC3
071-623 0444
Free. Mon-Fri 11.30-1.45
U Bank
Buses as for Bank Museum

Lloyd's of London, Lime Street, EC3
071-327 6210
Closed to all but pre-booked groups on Mon-Fri 10-12.30 & 2-3.45. Phone for latest information
U Bank, Cannon Street
BR Liverpool Street, Fenchurch Street, Cannon Street
Buses 15B, 22A, 25, 35, 47, 48, 505 along Cornhill
D

Monument, Monument Street, EC2
071-626 2717
Adults £1.00, Under 16 25p
April to September Mon-Fri 9-6, weekends 2-6 (last admissions 5.40); October to March Mon-Sat 9-4 (last admissions 3.40)
U Monument, Bank
Buses 15, 21, 22A, 25, 35, 40, 43, 44, 47, 48, 133, 214, 501, 505, 510, 513, D1

Tower Hill Pageant
Phone 071-924 2465 for up-to-date information, or contact the Museum of London on 071-600 3699
U Tower Hill
DLR Tower Gateway
Buses as Tower
D

Tower of London, Tower Hill, EC3
071-709 0765
Adults £5.90, 5-15 £3.70, Concessions £4.50
Free guided tours by the Yeoman Warders
March to October Mon-Sat 9.30-6.30 (last admissions at 5), Sun 2-6 (last admissions at 5); November to February Mon-Sat 9.30-4 (last admissions at 3)
Crown Jewels closed January
U Tower Hill
DLR Tower Gateway
Buses 15, X15, 25, 42, 78, 100, 510, D1
D Phone, limited

Tower Bridge, SE1
071-407 0922
Adults £2.50, Children & Senior citizens £1.00
April to October daily 10-6.30 (last admissions 5.45);
November to March daily 10-4.45 (last admissions at 4)
U Tower Hill, Docklands Light Railway
DLR Tower Gateway
Buses 42, 78 and 510 cross the bridge itself, other buses
as the Tower
D

ASTON'S ™

Aston's offer the most complete selection of accommodation, each range uniquely tailored to fit your budget and needs. Aston's is centrally located just minutes from Harrods, Hyde Park, Buckingham Palace, Theatres and museums. For reservations or more information please contact us. We'll look forward to your stay.

ASTON'S ™
BUDGET STUDIOS
From just
£25
a day

By combining self-catering convenience with elegant Victorian surroundings, our Aston's Budget Studios are quite simply the best of budget.

ASTON'S
DESIGNER STUDIOS ™
From just
£55
a day

We offer glorious designer decor, the best amenities and service. Marble Showers, Gold Fittings, Robes, Opulent Mirrors, Air Conditioning, Private Fax & Phone. Truly a luxury you can afford.

ASTON'S ™
LUXURY APARTMENTS
From just
£95
a day

Tired of hotels? Our luxury apartments are a charming combination of old world elegance and modern sophistication. Really a home away from home.

9 ROSARY GARDENS, LONDON SW7 4NQ
TEL: 071-370 0737 & 071-730 1100   FAX: 071-730 2382 & 071-835 1419

TOLL FREE (USA ONLY) 1 800 525 2810

E BEST IN THE
FOLLOW THE SIGNS
CARD BOOKINGS
867 1111

ALBERY THEATRE
St Martin's Lane
London WC2N 4AH
Box Office: 071 837 1115
⊖ Leicester Square

Y THEATRE
man Street
n W1V 8DY
1 867 1118
adilly Circus

COMEDY THEATRE
Panton Street
London SWIY 4DN
Box Office: 071 930 2578
⊖ Piccadilly Circus

L THEATRE
4 Whitehall
SW1A 2DY
1 867 1119
haring Cross

PHOENIX THEATRE
Charing Cross Road
London WC2H OJP
Box Office: 071 240 9661
⊖ Tottenham Court Road

MS THEATRE
Cross Road
WC2H ODA
1 867 1116
ester Square

MAYBOX GROUP PLC.
Albery Theatre
St Martin's Lane
London WC2N 4AH
Tel: 071 867 1122
Fax: 071 867 1131

SIDE TRIPS

So far the routes have stayed north of the Thames but there is much of interest south of the river, and along the river itself. From Waterloo mainline or tube station the South Bank arts complex can be explored. The **Hayward**

Museum of the Moving Image

Gallery is administered by the Arts Council and holds many shows of major importance in the arts world. The **Museum of the Moving Image** (MOMI) is an unashamed nostalgia trip for those who yearn for the golden age – or should it be silver age – of the cinema, while at the same time it displays the more exciting of the

National Film Theatre

newest techniques. Next door are the **National Film Theatre** and **National Theatre** and along the embankment is the **Royal Festival Hall**, a remnant of the 1951 Festival of Britain and the first building on this complex. The RFH has a cafeteria overlooking the river and Festival Pier.

Further inland there is more nostalgia at the **Imperial War Museum**. By the time you have gone back to Waterloo for a tube to Lambeth North, you might as well

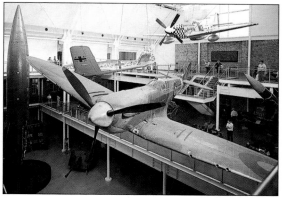

Imperial War Museum

walk to the museum, or perhaps just catch a bus heading down Waterloo Road. Go past the Old Vic theatre and the Imperial War Museum – the old Bethlehem (Bedlam) Hospital – dominates the next junction. Here you can experience life in the trenches, in the Blitz and in the Falklands.

If you want to explore the seedy side streets of historic **Southwark**, with its Shakespearean connections (William's brother Edmund was buried in Southwark Cathedral), the companion guides, *Budget London* and *Family London*, give further details.

After years of neglect the Thames is coming into its own again as a thoroughfare with the opening up of

National Theatre

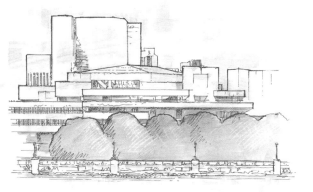

Docklands, and the RiverBus catamarans now slice through the Thames at speed every twenty minutes between Chelsea Harbour and the City Airport at the eastern end of the docks. The RiverBus stops at Charing Cross Pier, Festival Pier, Swan Lane (City) Pier, London Bridge Pier, West India (Docklands) Pier and Greenwich. All the piers are near tube stations and bus stops.

Westminster Pier, by Westminster tube station and bridge, is not a stop for the RiverBuses but for the traditional river cruisers. The leisurely trip upstream to **Hampton Court** goes first through Putney, the starting point of the Oxford and Cambridge boat race, then stops at **Kew**, the 300-acre botanical gardens along the Thames whose pagoda is its best-known landmark.

Richmond is next. By Richmond Bridge the complex of apparently eighteenth- and nineteenth-century houses with steps to the towpath, with the exception of the Italianate tower close to the bridge, was built in the 1980s. Richmond Hill rises to the left after the bridge, with extensive views of the river. (The song 'Lass of Richmond Hill' refers to Richmond in Yorkshire, a Georgian town well worth visiting if York is also on your

Richmond Bridge

Richmond Hill

agenda.) Perched on the top of the hill is the Royal Star and Garter Home for disabled ex-servicemen, who make the November poppies. Richmond Park, enclosed by Charles I for hunting, is on this side of the town with wild deer, horse-riders and the Isabella Plantation, which has to be seen in May for the azaleas and rhododendrons.

Hampton Court Palace

The Thames ceases to be a tidal river at Teddington Lock, further upstream. Teddington is well known to Londoners as the riverside home of Thames Television – the studios are on the river near the lock – but it was also the birthplace of Noel Coward, who lived there as a child. Nearby Kingston-upon-Thames was the coronation place of the Saxon kings and their coronation stone is outside the Guildhall.

The Maze

Hampton Court Palace presents its most magnificent frontage to the river so the approach by river is the best one for photographers. The palace was begun by Cardinal Wolsey who gave it to Henry VIII when he began to fear a fall from favour. William and Mary asked Wren to rebuild it to be the Versailles of London but his work remained uncompleted and some of the earlier palace fortunately remains. A major fire a few years ago destroyed some of its priceless treasures and the restoration work has itself become a tourist attraction. The gardens are also very fine, with a

Windsor Castle

maze that provides hours of innocent amusement. Turn left as you go in. Bushy Park, across the road from the palace, is tamer than Richmond Park but also has deer and horse-riding.

Further upstream is **Windsor** but it would be too much to do Hampton Court and Windsor on the same day. Windsor Castle must rank with the Tower of London among the greatest castles of the world. Since William the Conqueror built the first fortress here where the Round Tower now stands, kings and queens of England have made Windsor their second home. The Queen often stays here and, as at Buckingham Palace, the Royal Standard flies above the building when she is in residence — not the wisest of security measures. St George's Chapel is the resting place of most of the monarchs not buried in

Thames Barrier

Westminster Abbey — Henry VIII, Edward VI, Charles I, George III and Edward VII. Across the water is Eton College, founded in 1440. Its scholars are still distinguished by the black coats originally worn in mourning for George III. Set in the middle of the Thames is **Runnymede**, where King John signed the Magna Carta at the barons' command in 1215. London Coaches run river and coach trips to Hampton Court and Windsor; see their display advertisement.

Downstream from Westminster Pier the **Thames Barrier** at Woolwich has a visitor centre (on the south side of the river) with a cafe and

Cutty Sark

cruises round the barrier, which was built to protect London from flood tides before Docklands moved out eastwards beyond it.

Greenwich has the *Cutty Sark*, the old tea clipper, just across the dry dock from the tiny *Gypsy Moth IV*, in which Francis Chichester sailed around the world single-handed in 1966. The Queen appropriately knighted the lone yachtsman with the sword used by the earlier Elizabeth to knight the earlier Francis – Sir Francis Drake. The imposing **National Maritime Museum** is here with the Queen's House in its centre and the old **Royal Observatory**, with its round dome, at the top of the hill. At the observatory is the strip of brass set into stone which separates the western hemisphere from the eastern. Greenwich is to longitude what the equator is to latitude. It is also a lively village

National Maritime Museum

which never lets you forget its seafaring heritage.

Rather than get the bus or RiverBus back into London, why not go through the foot tunnel (via the lift) under the Thames? This links up with the Docklands Light Railway on the north side of the river, which is worth a separate visit just for the ride. It may seem alarming at first to ride in a driverless train – the system is completely automated – but the advantage is a driver's-eye view of the route through the redeveloping **Docklands**. Take the DLR from Island Gardens, the stop for Greenwich with its magnificent view of the National Maritime Museum across the river, to Shadwell and make for the church of **St George-in-the-East**, with its unmistakable Hawksmoor tower. The church is on the north side of the Highway, once Ratcliffe Highway and the scene of two horrific crimes in

Royal Observatory

1812. Across the Highway is Wapping Lane which leads to **Tobacco Dock**. Architecturally this is a most successful conversion from a unique warehouse built between 1811 and 1814. Commercially the dock, intended to be the Covent Garden piazza of east London, offers exciting possibilities.

The LDDC (London Docklands Development Corporation) has other retail schemes or (as they used to be called) shops, city farms, historic churches and museums, watersports and riverside pubs. The LDDC Visitors' Centre has information; see page 103.

The Museum in Docklands runs guided coach

St George-in-the-East

tours from the Museum of London on some Saturdays. The museum library and archives are open for research at other times. This is still in a formative phase. Watch the press or phone for details.

Tobacco Dock

Hayward Gallery, South Bank, SE1
071-928 3144, Recorded information 071-261 0127
Adults £4.00 (£2.50 on Mon), Concessions £2.50
Tue & Wed 10-8, Thur-Mon 10-6
U BR Waterloo
Buses (to Waterloo) 1, 4, 68, X68, 76, 149, 168, 171,
171A, 176, 188, 501, 502, 505, 507, 513, C1, D1, P11
D Phone

National Theatre, South Bank, SE1
071-928 2252
U BR Waterloo
Buses as for Hayward Gallery
D Phone

National Film Theatre, South Bank, SE1
071-928 3232
U BR Waterloo
Buses as for Hayward Gallery
D

Museum of the Moving Image, South Bank, SE1
071-928 3535, Recorded information 071-401 2636
Adults £4.95, Students £4.20, Children & Senior citizens
£3.50, Family (2+4 max) £15.00
Tue-Sat 10-8, Sun, Bank Holidays and half-term Mondays
10-6 (last admissions one hour before closing)
U BR Waterloo
Buses as for Hayward Gallery
D Phone

Imperial War Museum, Lambeth Road, SE1
071-416 5000, Recorded information 071-820 1283
Adults £3.00, 5-16 & Concessions £1.50, free on Fridays
Daily 10-6
U Lambeth North, Elephant and Castle
BR Waterloo, Elephant and Castle (from Waterloo)
Buses 1, 12, 44, 45, 53, 59, 63, 68, 141, 171, 176, 184,
188, 510
D Phone

Westminster Pier:
for Greenwich 071-930 4097; for Barrier 071-930 3373;
for Tower 071-930 9033; for upstream 071-930 4721

RiverBus: 071-512 0555

Docklands Light Railway: 071-222 1234

Hampton Court Palace
081-977 8441
Admission to palace and maze: Adults £4.50, 5-15 £2.80,
Concessions £3.40, Families £13.50
April to October daily 9.30-5.30
October to March last admissions at 4 pm
Park open 7 am to dusk daily
BR Hampton Court from Waterloo
Buses 715, 718
D

Royal Botanical Gardens, Kew
081-940 1171
Adults £3.00, 5-15 £1.00, Concessions £1.50
Daily from 9.30, closing time varies with daylight
U Kew Gardens
BR Kew Bridge (from Waterloo)
Buses 7, 27
D

Windsor Castle, Berks
0753 868286
Precincts: Daily except 14 June from 10.30, closing times
vary. Phone above number for current admission details or
phone Windsor Tourist Information Centre, 0753 852010

**Thames Barrier Visitors' Centre, Unity Way,
Woolwich, SE18**
081-854 1373
Adults £2.20, Under 16 & Concessions £1.35,
Families (2+3) £6.00
Daily 10.30-5
BR Charlton (from London Bridge)
Buses (to south side) 177

Cutty Sark, King William Walk, SE10

081-858 3445

Adults £2.50, Under 16 & Concessions £1.25 (children must be with an adult), Families (2+5 max) £6.00
April to September Mon-Sat 10-6, Sun 12-6;
October to March Mon-Sat 10-5, Sun 12-5
BR Greenwich, Maze Hill (from London Bridge)
DLR to Island Gardens then foot tunnel
Buses 1, 177, 188

Gypsy Moth IV, King William Walk, SE10

081-858 3445

Adults 50p, Under 16 30p
Easter to October daily 10-5.30 (last admissions); closed winter
BR Greenwich, Maze Hill (from London Bridge)
DLR Island Gardens then foot tunnel
Buses 1, 177, 188

National Maritime Museum, Romney Road, SE10

081-858 4422

Adults £3.20, Concessions £2.20
Greenwich 'passport' ticket to National Maritime Museum, Queen's House, Old Observatory and Cutty Sark, Adult £5.90, Concessions £3.90
April to September Mon-Sat 10-6, Sun 2-6; October to March Mon-Sat 10-5, Sun 2-5
BR Greenwich, Maze Hill (from London Bridge)
DLR Island Gardens then foot tunnel
Buses 1, 177, 188
D Limited, phone

Museum in Docklands (Museum of London)

071-515 1162

London Docklands Development Corporation Visitors' Centre, Limeharbour, Isle of Dogs

071-515 3000, ask for Visitors' Centre
Open daily
DLR Crossharbour, South Quays (Limeharbour runs north from the eastern end of Crossharbour and is also the site of the London Arena, a 12,000-seat sports and entertainment venue.)
Local buses D5, D6, P14

EVENINGS OUT

By night, London changes from a showpiece of history and pageantry into a glittering new world of culture and pleasure. There is, however, one ancient ceremony which is performed in the evening – the Ceremony of the Keys at the Tower of London. To witness this takes some organisation as you must write well in advance to the Governor of the Tower. But the lanterns in the darkness, the marching Yeoman Warders and the cry of the sentry as he challenges the Chief Warder's party: 'Halt, who goes there?' make this a unique experience.

The theatres which have today made London pre-eminent in the world as a centre of both serious drama and showbiz entertainment are often historic in their own

London Coliseum

right. The best way to view them is to attend a show, but a quick visit to some after-dark exteriors can make a tour in itself. The Theatre Royal, Drury Lane, was once one of only two theatres allowed in London by Charles II. (The other became the Royal Opera House, Covent Garden.) Today's building, rebuilt in 1794, has seen Irving, Ivor Novello and Dan Leno as well as most of the great post-war stage shows from 'Oklahoma' to 'Miss Saigon'.

The Royal Opera House, in an earlier form, premiered Goldsmith's 'She Stoops to Conquer' and Sheridan's 'The Rivals'. It was rebuilt after fires in 1858.

The London Coliseum, in St Martin's Lane, the giant among London theatres – seating 2358 – is the home of the English National Opera. The theatre's founder, Oswald Stoll, had a mobile lounge on tracks installed to whisk royal parties straight to their box, and this was the first theatre in London to have a revolving stage. He also insisted on 'No swearing' notices in all dressing rooms and installed a bust of his mother in the vestibule. The globe on top originally span round.

In Haymarket two veterans face each other. The Theatre Royal, originally dating from 1720, was redesigned by Nash and opened in 1821. Her Majesty's, opposite, was rebuilt in 1897. The Theatre Royal achieved new fame as the home of Oscar Wilde's comedies, and across the road Her Majesty's was the home of the great Henry Beerbohm Tree's spectacular Shakespeare productions. As I write, the 'Phantom of the Opera' here is fully booked for the foreseeable future.

Other long runners are 'The Mousetrap', at St Martin's – the longest runner of them all, since November 1952 – 'Les Misérables' at the Palace, 'Aspects of Love' at the Prince of Wales and 'Cats' at the New London. Daily papers have full listings and booking details. Half-price tickets can be bought at the kiosk in Leicester Square for the night's performance. This is not a shady operation – it is run by the Society of West End Theatre.

For an evening stroll, why not brave the former royal hunting ground of Soho? It still has traces of being London's old Latin quarter, and it is not as wicked as it looks at first. Behind the gaudy signs, the orange light bulbs and flashing red signs there is some fine architecture and plenty of historic ghosts. Karl Marx lived at 26 Dean Street (now Leoni's Quo Vadis Restaurant) and Canaletto stayed at 41 Beak Street during his visit to London to produce his lovely Thames pictures. Broadwick Street was once the home of William Blake, the painter and poet, and of Daniel Defoe, author of *Robinson Crusoe*.

Gerrard Street is now a suburb of Hong Kong rather than an ordinary London street. Signs in Chinese characters – and often menus as well – proclaim this the heart of Chinatown. But Dryden once lived here at Number 43, Edmund Burke at Number 37 and Boswell at one time at Number 22.

You don't have to be a hardened drinker to want to visit London's historic pubs and eating houses. They offer an inexpensive nightlife among the ghosts of the past.

The Lamb & Flag in Rose Street, Covent Garden, was known as the 'Bucket of Blood' during the rough-house days of past centuries. It was here that Dryden was roughed up for writing rude verses. The Salisbury, 90 St Martin's Lane, is a good solid theatreland pub representative of many in this area.

For central eating Covent Garden hums into the early hours. Try the Ivy, at 1 West Street, for a special meal (071-836 4751). For a more informal evening try the Cafe Pacifico, off Long Acre, for Mexican food and sangria in a converted warehouse.

If you're north of centre, the Olde Bull and Bush, North End Way, Hampstead, immortalised in the old music hall song, is still a popular Hampstead pub. West of centre try the Bunch of Grapes, 207 Brompton Road, Chelsea. South of the river the George Inn, down a tiny yard off Borough High Street, is London's last galleried coaching inn. Eastwards can be found many once sinister riverside pubs on both sides of the river. The most famous is the Prospect of Whitby, Wapping, formerly the haunt of Whistler and Turner.

Royal National Theatre

~~Gallery~~

~~River Terraces~~

~~Bookshop~~

Backstage Tours

~~Restaurant~~

~~Live Music~~

~~Cafe~~

Some theatre.

The Royal National Theatre is like no other - there's so much to choose from. Within its walls the National's three theatres offer a choice of internationally acclaimed work, both classic and modern. From our riverside terraces you can sit and enjoy the panoramic sweep of London, its historic landmarks and timeless river.

We also have free foyer concerts and exhibitions, a first class theatre Bookshop, backstage tours, a restaurant and cafés open all day.

The National (it became 'Royal' in 1988) has its own special place in London's history. Its artistic foundations were laid over 100 years ago but it was not until 1973 that Laurence Olivier, our first director and namesake of our largest stage, brought the company to its current home on the South Bank. Its actors, directors and writers have been making theatre history ever since. Phone 071-633 0880 and we'll bring you up to date.

ROYAL NATIONAL THEATRE,
SOUTH BANK, LONDON SE1 9PX
FOYERS OPEN 10am - 11pm
MONDAY-SATURDAY.

NT

ROYAL NATIONAL THEATRE

TRADITIONAL EVENTS

The London Tourist Board (LTB) publishes a list of traditional events each January to help plan your trip to the capital. Phone LTB on 071-730 3488 for exact dates. For events in the City call in or phone the information bureau in St Paul's Churchyard on 071-606 3030. Acknowledgements to LTB for supplying the information below (in October 1990). Note that all guidebooks are out of date in some respects by the time they appear, so do check with the relevant tourist body before setting out.

DAILY

Changing the guard: Horse guards leave their barracks in Hyde Park 10.28 am Mon-Sat, 9.28 am Sun, for the ceremony at Horse Guards, Whitehall, at 11 am Mon-Sat, 10 am Sun. Changing the guard at Buckingham Palace is 11.30 daily April to end July and alternate days from August to approximately end March (not in wet weather).

NIGHTLY

Ceremony of the Keys: Tower. Write for tickets to the Governor, Tower of London, EC3N 4AB, with as many alternative dates as possible.

JANUARY

Royal Epiphany Gifts Service: 6 January at Chapel Royal, St James's Palace, SW1.

Charles I Commemoration: Last Sunday at Banqueting House and Trafalgar Square, midday.

FEBRUARY

Chinese New Year: Dates vary for celebrations in Soho. Gun salute: 6 February. Commemorates Queen's accession to throne. Hyde Park at noon, Tower at 1 pm. (If 6 February is a Sunday, guns are fired on following Monday.)

MARCH

Oxford and Cambridge University Boat Race: On a Saturday on the Thames between Putney Bridge and Mortlake.

Bridewell Thanksgiving Service: Second Tuesday at St Bride's church, Fleet Street. Lord Mayor of London, in robes, attends service at noon.

Oranges and Lemons Service: Third or fourth Thursday at church of St Clement Danes in the Strand, 3 pm.

Spring Equinox: Druids celebrate the equinox on Tower Hill at noon.

EASTER

Maundy Money: In 1991 this ceremony is at Westminster Abbey, but it moves to a different place each year.

Butterworth Charity: Morning service at St Bartholomew-the-Great, Smithfield, concludes with distribution of money and hot cross buns.

Easter Parade: Easter Sunday in Battersea Park.

Harness Horse Parade: Easter Monday in Regent's Park.

APRIL

Spital Sermon: First Thursday after Easter at St Lawrence Jewry-next-Guildhall. Lord Mayor, sheriffs, aldermen in procession from Guildhall, noon.

Stow Commemoration: St Andrew Undershaft, Leadenhall Street, EC3. Date varies.

Gun salute: 21 April, Queen's birthday (as February).

Tyburn Walk: Silent procession from Old Bailey to Marble Arch, last Sunday.

MAY

Historic Commercial Vehicle Run: First Sunday at Crystal Palace Park from 6.30 am.

Epsom Derby: First Wednesday on Epsom Downs, Surrey.

Dunkirk Veterans' Service: St Lawrence Jewry-next-Guildhall, EC2, 3pm. Date varies.

London Private Fire Brigades' target spraying competition: Guildhall Yard, noon on a May Saturday, also on a date in September.

Punch and Judy Festival: Covent Garden, followed by service at St Paul's, Covent Garden, second Sunday at 11 am.

Beating the Bounds: All Hallows-by-the-Tower, Ascension Day (sixth Thursday after Easter), 3 pm.

Every three years also at St Peter ad Vincula in the Tower, 6 pm.

Chelsea Flower Show: Late May at the Royal Hospital, Chelsea. Phone 071-828 1744 for recorded details.

JUNE

Trooping the Colour: Second Sunday in June to celebrate the Queen's official birthday. Horse Guards Parade, 11 am. Write for a maximum of two tickets before the end of February to the Brigade Major (Trooping the Colour), Headquarters, Household Division, Horse Guards, SW1A 2AX.

Beating Retreat and Sounding Retreat: In June on Horse Guards Parade. Tickets from the end of February from Premier Box Office, 1b Bridge Street, SW1A 2JR, 071-839 6815/071-836 4114.

Royal Ascot: Towards the end of June. Tickets from the Secretary, Grandstand, Ascot, Berks.

Gun salute: 10 June for birthday of Prince Philip. See February for details.

Pepys Commemoration Service: St Olave's church, Hart Street, EC3R 7NB. Write to the church for details of the service and the buffet lunch.

Election of sheriffs: Around midsummer at Guildhall. Write in advance for tickets to the Keeper, Guildhall, EC2P 2EJ.

JULY

Royal Tournament: Mid-July at Earl's Court. The Queen and other senior members of the Royal Family take the salute. Write from mid-March to Royal Tournament Box Office, Earl's Court Exhibition Centre, Warwick Road, SW5 9TA.

Royal Tournament

AUGUST

Gun salute: 4 August for the Queen Mother's birthday. See February for details.

Cart Marking Ceremony: Guildhall Yard at midday.

London Riding Horse Parade: First Sunday in August, Rotten Row. Phone LTB for the address of the current secretary of the parade to obtain entry form and details.

Notting Hill Carnival: August Bank Holiday and the Sunday before it.

SEPTEMBER

Autumn Equinox: Druids hold equinox celebrations at Primrose Hill.

Election of Lord Mayor: 29 September, or near, at Guildhall. Tickets from the Keeper, Guildhall, EC2P 2EJ.

Punch and Judy Festival: Covent Garden.

OCTOBER

Judges' Service: First weekday in October, Westminster Abbey. Private function but procession to Parliament at about 11.45.

Pearly Harvest Festival: First Sunday at St Martin-in-the-Fields, Trafalgar Square, 3 pm.

Vintage Festival: St Olave's, Hart Street, EC3.

Harvest of the Sea: Second Sunday in October at either St Mary-at-Hill, EC3, or St Margaret Pattens, Rood Lane.

National Service for Seafarers: Nearest Wednesday to Trafalgar Day, 21 October, St Paul's Cathedral, 6 pm. Tickets from Hon. Sec., Annual National Service for Seafarers, St Michael Paternoster Royal, College Hill, EC4R 2RL.

NOVEMBER

Fireworks Night: Yeomen of the Guard still check the cellars of the Houses of Parliament prior to the State Opening of Parliament and all around the country bonfires and firework displays are held on or near 5 November. Phone 071-730 3488 in October for London firework displays.

State Opening of Parliament: Early to mid-November. Not open to public but usually on television. Procession from Buckingham Palace at approximately 11 am.

London to Brighton Veteran Car Run: First Sunday in November. Starts Hyde Park Corner 8-9 am.

Lord Mayor's Show: Second Saturday of November. Procession in City from 11 am.

Remembrance Sunday Ceremony: Second Sunday in November, Cenotaph, Whitehall, 11 am.

DECEMBER

Boar's Head Presentation: Procession to Mansion House, in the City. Date varies.

CHRISTMAS

Christmas lights: Switched on in Regent Street and Oxford Street in mid-November.

New Year's Eve: Midnight in crowded Trafalgar Square, or Parliament Square to hear Big Ben ring in the new year.

Christmas lights

Bank Holidays	1991	1992
New Year's Day	1 January	1 January
Good Friday	29 March	17 April
Easter Monday	1 April	20 April
May Day Bank Holiday	6 May	4 May
Spring Bank Holiday	27 May	25 May
August Bank Holiday	26 August	31 August
Christmas Day	25 December	25 December
Boxing Day	26 December	28 December

USING LONDON'S PUBLIC TRANSPORT

When you visit London, the best way to get around is the Londoners' way – by public transport. Central London and the suburbs are well served by both bus and Underground networks, and the fully wheelchair accessible Docklands Light Railway has opened up the Thames-side areas east of the Tower.

The headquarters of London Transport (LT) is at 55 Broadway, SW1, above St James's Park tube station, which also houses the London Transport Travel Shop. This deals not only with tickets and London Transport enquiries but sells a wide range of LT merchandise, souvenirs and books. In addition, there are Travel Information Centres at the following Underground stations: St James's Park, King's Cross, Liverpool Street, Oxford Circus, Piccadilly Circus and Heathrow. There are other LT Travel Information Centres at Victoria station and Euston British Rail station, at West Croydon bus station and at all Heathrow terminals. See the London Transport services section for further details. Phone 071-222 1234 for travel enquiries and Travelcheck on 071-222 1200 for regularly updated travel information.

UNDERGROUND

The **Underground**, or tube, is the most comprehensive subway network in the world. It's fast and convenient – unless you're in a wheelchair. If this is the case see Disabled in London section for advice on transport in London. There are eleven Underground lines including the Docklands Light Railway, each with its own colour code. See the journey planner on the back cover. Smoking is banned everywhere on the Underground system.

DOCKLANDS LIGHT RAILWAY

The **Docklands Light Railway** (DLR) was opened in 1987, and runs in a Y-shape from Tower Gateway and Stratford down to a terminus at Island Gardens on the Isle of Dogs, where there is a DLR visitor centre. Extensions are planned to Bank in the City and to Beckton, beyond the eastern Royal Docks.

The service is fully automated with trains running

every few minutes. The main station is at Tower Gateway where there is a small information office (open 10–4 Mon–Fri only). Ticket machines take coins rather than notes so be sure to have plenty of change. Travelcards are valid on the service (see overleaf for details).

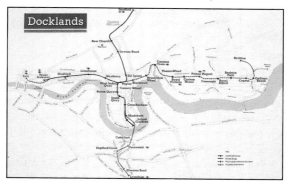

BUSES

Buses are no longer all red but those that aren't can be recognised as part of the London Transport system by the familiar roundel that they all carry. If you are sightseeing you may not want to go the fastest way, by tube, choosing instead to catch some sights on the way. Buses to the central attractions covered in this book are indicated in the in-

dividual chapters. If you take the number 11, for example, it will take you from Liverpool Street station through the City, past St Paul's, Trafalgar Square, Westminster Abbey and down the King's Road to Chelsea. Or try the number 188 from Euston, which goes to Greenwich via the British Museum and the South Bank arts complex, and passes close to Tower Bridge. Free bus maps and guides are obtainable at LT's Travel Information Centres.

Buses have their own intriguing history. For instance, the bottom deck of a double-decker is still called 'inside', recalling the days when the top was open to the weather. See the London Transport Museum in Covent Garden for their fascinating collection of historic vehicles, posters and memorabilia.

Most **bus stops** in central London are named on the

post or shelter and carry travel information. There are two kinds of stops: the compulsory stop, red on a white background, and the request stop, white on a red background. To hail the bus put out an arm. The driver will not stop if the bus is full.

Sometimes it's wise to hail a bus at the compulsory stop, especially at night, in case the driver hasn't seen you.

Buses with a conductor are double-deckers (usually boarded at the back) and the conductor will tell you where to get off if you ask. Ring the bell in good time just once to tell the driver to stop. Driver-only-operated buses (both single- and double-deckers) are boarded at the front.

Red Arrows are single-deck buses (501-513) running mainly between British Rail stations. They are driver-operated buses with a flat fare, currently 70p. Exact money is needed and the driver cannot give change.

Carelink and **Mobility** Buses are run by LT for the disabled, see Disabled in London section for details.

Night buses all pass through Trafalgar Square and serve main cinema, restaurant and theatre areas in central London until the day buses start. They have an N in front of the route number. For full details phone 071-222 1234.

BUYING YOUR TICKET

One-journey bus tickets are bought on the bus and one-journey single or return tickets on the tube are bought at the station of departure. Keep your ticket until the end of the journey in case an inspector is travelling on your route.

London is divided into six travel zones, from zone 1 in the central area to zone 6 in the suburbs. Bus passes are available in different combinations of zones for a week, a month or three months. They are valid at any time of day and are used by London's commuters. Buy them from certain bus garages, selected newsagents and Travel Information Centres. You will need to take a passport-type photograph along with you.

One-day, 7-day, monthly and 3-monthly Travelcards are valid for bus, Mobility Bus, tube and DLR, and for

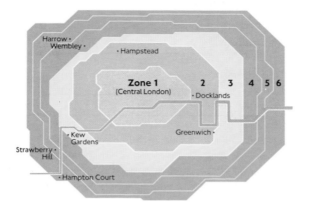

Network SouthEast (the British Rail suburban system). They are not valid on the Airbus or on guided coach tours. The 1-day Travelcards are valid after 9.30 am on Mondays to Fridays, and all day at weekends. They are not valid on the night buses. Travelcards are for sale at tube stations, Travel Information Centres and some newsagents. For all Travelcards except the 1-day you will need to present a passport-type photo when you buy.

AUTOMATIC MACHINES

There are self-service **ticket machines** in most tube stations to save a long wait. Follow the instructions on the

machines. The larger style of machine displays the prices and zones. The smaller machine can be used if you know the fare. Both types accept coins from the 5p piece to the £1 and give change. The larger machine accepts the £5 note in good condition. Be sure to keep plenty of change to hand. **Ticket gates** are also automated. To enter the tube system slide the ticket with the wording uppermost into the slot on the right-hand side of the gate. The gate opens when you remove your ticket. Leave the station in the same way – the ticket is returned to you if it is valid for another journey.

GETTING TO THE AIRPORT

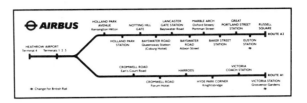

The wheelchair accessible **Airbus** links the major hotel areas with **Heathrow** every half-hour from approximately 6.30 am until 8 pm. The tube (Piccadilly line) also links central London with Heathrow, and the journey takes about an hour. At night, bus N97 runs hourly between central London and Heathrow.

Gatwick is served by the Gatwick Express from Victoria British Rail station every 15 minutes from 5.30 am to 10 pm. The journey time is 30 minutes non-stop. Less frequent trains run overnight. You can check your luggage in at Victoria for some flights from Gatwick; ring first to find out (0293 31299).

DISABLED IN LONDON

It is possible to see many of the sights of London with careful advance planning. Most major museums and tourist attractions are improving their facilities for the disabled all the time and welcome wheelchairs, especially if you telephone first. Madame Tussaud's have to limit the number of wheelchairs they permit in case of fire, so do phone there before you set out. Phone numbers are given in the information sections for each itinerary.

Getting into London from Heathrow is not difficult by wheelchair as there are frequent wheelchair accessible **Airbuses** from Heathrow to Victoria and Euston stations that stop at several hotels on routes A1 and A2. Phone London Transport (LT) on 071-222 1234 for travel information. Leave out the 071 prefix if you are dialling from a number that has an 071 prefix.

The clockwise **Carelink** wheelchair bus run by LT runs hourly every day and connects up seven main railway termini: Euston, St Pancras, King's Cross, Liverpool Street, Waterloo, Victoria and Paddington. The driver may be able to make extra stops with advance notice as long as the timetable can be kept to. Phone LT's Unit for Disabled Passengers on 071-222 5600 for further information.

LT run **Mobility Buses** regularly to help the disabled in the suburbs do their shopping. Standard bus fares are charged as if the service were a regular bus. The most useful bus for visitors is Route 925 which runs on Wednesdays only from the East End. It arrives at Tower Gateway at 10.20 and stops at Liverpool Street, King's Cross, Euston, Oxford Circus, Marble Arch, Hyde Park Corner and Victoria station (at 11.40). The return trip leaves the Wilton Road coach station (Victoria) at 13.45 and arrives back at Liverpool Street at 15.00 before heading out to the East End. Phone 071-222 5600 for details.

The **Original London Transport Sightseeing Tour** has special wheelchair accessible tours from Wilton Road coach station (Victoria) on Saturdays, Mondays and Thursdays. Phone 071-828 7395 for information and booking.

The **Docklands Light Railway** (DLR) is completely automated with trains that are fully accessible for wheelchairs (two per train). An emergency button on the trains and platforms connects with the control room in case of difficulties. Automatic ticket machines take coins rather than notes, so be sure to have plenty of change on you. Travelcards are valid on the DLR as it is part of LT. Note that the 925 Mobility Bus stops at Tower Gateway DLR station on Wednesdays. Travel enquiries on the usual LT number 071-222 1234 (queuing system so hang on); leaflets from 071-222 5600.

The **Underground** is the least preferred option by wheelchair users and non-folding wheelchairs cannot be accommodated at all times on many sections. LT publish *Access to the Underground* to help, but steps are everywhere.

Disabled **car parking** is available in several places on the outer edges of inner London. Phone *Tripscope* on 081-994 9294 in office hours for free information on getting around anywhere in London. There are several useful phone numbers for the disabled in London (see below for a selection), but with the charity *Tripscope* you tap into the 'disability mafia' – the network of London disabled who know all the wheezes and short cuts because they live here.

Roving **taxis** are becoming more and more wheelchair accessible, especially from ranks where the adapted cabs are more easily spotted. If you are unlucky try the following numbers and ask for a taxi which can take a wheelchair, giving as much notice as possible:

Black Radio Taxis	081-209 0266
Data Cab	071-727 7200
Computer Cab	071-286 7009
Lords Radio Taxis	071-253 5000
Radio Taxis	071-272 0272

or phone *Tripscope* (who kindly provided these numbers) for an up-to-date list.

An independent guide to getting around London is *Access in London*, published by Nicholson in 1989, which has details of steps and toilets and much more.

For a RADAR key to disabled toilets and other information phone in office hours or write to the Royal Association for Disability and Rehabilitation (RADAR), 25 Mortimer Street, W1, 071-637 5400.

Other useful numbers are: Disabled Living Foundation, 071-289 6111; Greater London Association for the Disabled (GLAD), 071-274 0107; Disability Action Westminster, 071-630 5994; and Artsline (for arts and entertainment access), 071-388 2227.

LT's Unit for Disabled Passengers will send a comprehensive package of up-to-date London Transport information (in large print or on cassette if wished). Phone 071-222 5600 in office hours or write to them at 55 Broadway, SW1H 0BD. The London Transport Museum, in the corner of Covent Garden, is fully accessible for wheelchairs, with free admission for the disabled and their helpers.

LONDON TRANSPORT SERVICES

The **Travel Information Service** is London Transport's shop window. It exists to provide passengers and potential passengers with helpful advice and guidance about every aspect of travelling around London – by bus, by tube, by the Docklands Light Railway and by British Rail. It can also give general information about the London tourist scene. Details of the location and opening times of Travel Information Centres are given below. Alternatively ring 071-222 1234.

TRAVEL INFORMATION CENTRES

These are open at Underground stations, Heathrow Airport and West Croydon bus station as follows:

	Mon-Fri	Saturday	Sunday
Euston (BR Concourse)	07.15-18.00 (to 19.30 Fri)	07.15-18.00	08.15-18.00
King's Cross	08.15-18.00 (to 19.30 Fri)	08.15-18.00	08.15-18.00
Liverpool Street	09.30-18.30	08.30-18.30	08.30-15.30
Oxford Circus	08.15-18.00	08.15-18.00	CLOSED
Piccadilly Circus	08.15-18.00	08.15-18.00	08.15-18.00
St James's Park	09.00-17.30	CLOSED	CLOSED
Victoria (BR Concourse – opposite Platform 8)	08.15-21.30	08.15-21.30	08.15-21.30
Heathrow 1,2,3 (station)	07.15-18.30	07.15-18.30	08.15-18.30
Heathrow Terminal 1	07.15-22.15	07.15-21.00	08.15-22.00
Heathrow Terminal 2	07.15-21.00	07.15-21.00	08.15-22.00
Heathrow Terminal 3	06.30-13.15	06.30-13.15	08.15-15.00
Heathrow Terminal 4	06.30-18.30	06.30-18.30	08.15-18.30

West Croydon bus station

Mon 07.00-19.00, Tue-Fri 07.30-18.30, Sat 08.00-18.30, Sun closed

24-hour travel information: 071-222 1234

Travelcheck recorded information: 071-222 1200

For information by post, write to Travel Information Service, London Transport, 55 Broadway, London SW1H 0BD.

Free maps and leaflets Tourist information folders and Underground maps, along with a range of other free leaflets, are available at Travel Information Centres and most hotels.

Bargain Tickets and Tourist Services Ask at Underground stations and Travel Information Centres for prices and availability of Travelcards and bus passes.

The Original London Transport Sightseeing Tour and **Official guided coach tours** See page 125 and ask for free leaflets at Travel Information Centres.

London Transport Museum, The Piazza, Covent Garden; open daily except 24, 25 and 26 December 10 am to 6 pm (last admission 5.15 pm). Come and see the many colourful and historic displays including horse buses, motor buses, trams, trolleybuses and railway vehicles. The museum shop (entrance free) stocks a wide range of books, posters, postcards and unusual souvenirs.

USING THE TELEPHONE

Central London numbers begin with the prefix 071- and outer London numbers begin with 081-. Central London is the area within four miles of Charing Cross. You do not need to dial the prefix if the number you are phoning from already has the same prefix. If you have any difficulty dial 100 and the operator will help you.

Phone boxes take 10p, 20p, 50p and £1 coins and the display tells you to 'insert coin' before you begin to dial. Unused coins are returned. Some phone boxes take phonecards only. These can be bought from post offices and newsagents' shops and cost £2, £4, £10 and £20. If you want directory enquiries dial 142 for London postal addresses and 192 for other British addresses. If you are phoning abroad dial 190 for general enquiries or 153 for directory enquiries. The direct dialling code out of Britain begins 010-.

Some telephone boxes now take credit cards. Instructions are displayed in the individual boxes.

HELP IN AN EMERGENCY

For emergencies dial 999 for police, fire brigade or ambulance. The call is free from any telephone.

Bliss chemists at Marble Arch are open till midnight every day of the week. Their telephone number is 071-723 6116.

British Transport Police, for reporting crimes on London Transport, are on 071-222 5600.

If you need hospital treatment in central London try University College Hospital, Gower Street, WC1; Middlesex Hospital, Mortimer Street, W1; St Mary's Hospital, Praed Street, W2; St Thomas' Hospital, Lambeth Palace Road, SE1, or Westminster Hospital, Horseferry Road, SW1.

Emergency dental treatment can be obtained at a charge from the Emergency Dental Service, 081-677 6363.

Property lost on buses or tubes may find its way to the Lost Property Office at 200 Baker Street, NW1 5RZ, near Baker Street tube station. The office is open on Mondays to Fridays 9.30 to 2 pm. For lost property recorded information ring 071-486 2496. For other lost property apply to the nearest police station.

TOURIST INFORMATION

London Tourist Board and Convention Bureau
26 Grosvenor Gardens, SW1W 0DU, 071-730 3450

Information centres at:
Victoria station Forecourt
SW1: open Easter to October daily 9-8.30 pm; November
to Easter Mon-Sat 9-7 pm, Sun 9-5 pm

Harrods
Knightsbridge, SW1 (fourth floor): open during store
hours

Heathrow Airport
Terminals 1, 2, 3, Underground station Concourse: open
daily 9-6 pm; Terminal 2 Arrivals Concourse, open daily
9-7 pm

Selfridges
Oxford Street, W1 (Basement Services Arcade); open
during store hours

Tower of London
West Gate, EC3; open Easter to October daily 10-6 pm

Telephone information service
071-730 3488 Mon-Fri 9-6 pm (automatic queuing
system)

British Travel Centre
12 Regent Street, Piccadilly Circus, SW1Y 4PQ,
071-730 3400: open Mon-Fri 9-6.30 pm, Sat & Sun 10-4
pm (extended in summer)

City of London Information Centre
St Paul's Churchyard, EC4, 071-606 3030, for
information relating to the square mile of the City of
London: open May to September daily 9.30-5 pm;
October to April Mon-Fri 9.30-5 pm, Sat 9.30-12 noon.

Bureaux de Change
Banks are normally open Mon-Fri 9.30-3.30 pm. Other
exchange facilities can be found at mainline railway
stations, central Underground stations and in some larger
department stores. They may have longer opening hours
than banks.

THE ORIGINAL LONDON TRANSPORT SIGHTSEEING TOUR

Take an introductory look at London with the Original London Transport Sightseeing Tour – open top in good weather. You pass all the major central London attractions: Tower Bridge, Tower, St Paul's Cathedral, Piccadilly Circus, Trafalgar Square, Houses of Parliament and Big Ben, travelling along some of London's famous streets: Fleet Street, Strand, Park Lane and around Hyde Park Corner.

Guided tours in English go from Piccadilly Circus (Haymarket, Stop L), Victoria station (Victoria Street, Stop T) and Marble Arch (Park Lane, Stop Z) every 30 minutes daily from 10 am until 4 pm (except at 1.30 pm).

A tour with taped commentary in English, Dutch, French, German, Italian, Japanese, Spanish and Swedish leaves the forecourt of Baker Street Underground station at the same times. Note that the times shown are only a guide and are subject to alteration to meet demand. Where possible, the departures on the hour are maintained.

Combined tickets to save queuing at Madame Tussaud's, London Zoo and Rock Circus are available from sales agents listed below and from departure points, except that the Madame Tussaud's ticket is not sold at Baker Street:

- Porters' desks at many hotels
- London Coaches Wilton Road coach station, Victoria
- London Transport Travel Information Centres
- London Tourist Board Information Centres
- American Express Desk at the British Travel Centre, 12 Regent Street W1.

Tours information
071-227 3456.
For wheelchair accessible tours see the Disabled in London section or phone 071-828 7395.

OFFICIAL GUIDED COACH TOURS

Because London Transport knows the best way to see the sights, they have assembled an exciting programme of guided tours, carefully selected to show you places that have played an important part in England's history.

On each tour you travel in a modern luxury coach and

are escorted by a friendly and experienced guide who has an expert knowledge of the places you will visit, and is approved to the high standard of the London Tourist Board.

A London Transport guided tour is a wonderful day out. On each day tour you can enjoy a relaxing lunch, and the price of all tours includes admissions charges.

SUMMER PROGRAMME
London Tours

Day tours

Westminster and City including changing of the guard and the Tower; river tour to Hampton Court Palace.

Morning tours

Westminster and changing of the guard.

Sunday luncheon cruise

Sights of London/changing of the guard/lunch cruising to Greenwich.

Afternoon tours

City of London; river cruise to Hampton Court Palace or Windsor.

Evening tours

Romance of London including dinner cruise; escorted theme evenings.

Country Tours

Day tours

Leeds Castle; Stonehenge, Longleat and Bath; Stratford, Oxford, Bladon and the Cotswolds; Stratford and Warwick Castle; Boulogne.

Extended tours

Visit England's lovely cathedral cities and towns, Lake District, Stonehenge, Bath, Shakespeare country, Devon and Cornwall, Scotland, Wales and Ireland.

Tours pick up from most major hotels. For full details ask for a free leaflet at Travel Information Centres or phone 071-222 1234.

BEWARE OF PICKPOCKETS

Keep an eye on your money and credit cards in crowded areas. Men should know how foolish it is to put wallets in their back trouser pockets. Beware of being jostled in a queue as some pickpockets work in groups. Women should beware of bag snatchers. Thieves watch you withdraw cash then follow you discreetly. Sooner or later your attention slips and the bag disappears. Hook your bag handle round your ankle in restaurants and hang it on a hook in the Ladies if there is a gap under the door. Another villainous trick is to slice through shoulder bag straps with a razor-blade.

Always lock your car and hide valuables under the seat or in the boot (trunk). Don't drive with a handbag or camera on the passenger seat if the window is open. Enterprising thieves on bikes can hook them away and leave you fuming in the traffic.

LONDON TRANSPORT MUSEUM SHOP PRESENTS LINES THAT GO ON AND ON

There are many gift shops in London, few however, are as varied and interesting as ours. There's something for everyone from five to ninety-five. From Aberdeen to Zagreb, Paris to Pittsburg. Old ticket machines to highest quality English Crystal. Tube map mugs, beautiful poster art books to transport magazines, children's toys and fine models. We present the best of London and its transport. With so much to offer it's no wonder we say our lines go on and on.

New Line

Posters

Games

T-shirts

Videos

Ever
Changing

Books

Cards

Models

Gifts

Souvenirs

London Transport Museum Shop.
Open 7 days a week 10.00 to 18.00.

The Piazza, Covent Garden, London WC2

FOR YOUR PERSONAL USE